Love Unconditional

Peter F. Simpson

authorHOUSE™

1663 Liberty Drive, Suite 200
Bloomington, Indiana 47403
(800) 839-8640
www.AuthorHouse.com

First published by AuthorHouse 09/14/05

ISBN: 1-4208-7264-8 (sc)

Printed in the United States of America
Bloomington, Indiana

This book is printed on acid-free paper.

*Friendship needs to win approval
         but love once given is unconditional.*

PROLOGUE

Honoured by his President, well known both in Guyana and among the Guyanese community in London, Vincent was manipulative and domineering but at the same time extremely popular.

After Vincent died and I went to stay with Sugar and Kenneth I began to hear rumours about the way he died and my part in it.

A woman who had never met either of us visited Sugar early one morning and started to tell her all about a black man who had died recently. While he was in the process of dying the white man that lived with him had beaten him and then ripped all the rings off of his fingers and taken all his valuables.

Sugar was furious with the woman, outraged she told the woman exactly what had happened and then asked her to leave the house. Shortly after that I myself met someone who repeated most of these allegations especially about the beatings. I showed her the scars that are still visible on my head and let her know that Vincent had given all his jewellery away while he lay dying except for the two rings that he had given to me, one for my brother and one for me. After the funeral everyone who had been given rings and gold chains came to me and asked me what they should do. I answered that if he had given them, they should keep them; after all that's what he wanted and they were of no significance to me, I had come to the conclusion that mere things cannot do anything for us, they certainly couldn't keep us alive.

These events prompted me to write down my own version of our life together so that there could be no mistake. At first I wrote about the ending of our life together and wrote about 20 pages but it didn't seem enough and so I decided to start at the beginning.

CHAPTER ONE.

When the sun shines through the open door and the jazz programme on the radio is Playing one of those classic love songs, the scent of the garden reminds me of Australia. I take another glass of rum and let the memories flood my brain. I remember that Les never liked to hear Deep Purple even when sang by Nat King Cole, which I loved. Maybe it's not quite jazz but the tunes they play remind me of it. Les died in the Spring and I thought then that my life had come to an end. I didn't know then that it was just a part of my life that had finished and a new life was just around the corner. We had been together for 3 years and had everything that I always thought mattered; a comfortable house with well-stocked cupboards, a blue Volkswagon, money to spend and of course each other. Les was such a nice man, tall and handsome with dark hair going grey and an air of easy confidence that endeared him to everyone he met. I loved going out with him to restaurants where his confident manner ensured instant recognition and the quick service he expected and received naturally. No-one was in any doubt , here was a gentleman. We were considered a most unusual couple by most of our friends in Melbourne, after all 3 years was a long time when most liasions staggered precariously on the brink, collapsing after a month or two and most frequently within weeks of the first rapturous declarations of love.

Les had always been a drinker, I tried to keep down his consumption of alcohol by meeting him when he left work and suggesting that we have a drink together and then making sure that we went home early to eat. I had been pretty successful but about a month before he died he managed to evade my watchful eye and began to drink even more heavily. He took time off work and seemed to just disappear.

He would come home late in the evening or early morning absolutely drunk, in addition to this he was also using phenobarbitone which he told me was for tiredness. "This is just like a tonic" he said "perfectly harmless, try one or two it will buck you up." I didn't try them then, but later on was prescribed them and then when back in London I combined them with alcohol with some horrific effects.

One hot morning when the sun shone and the temperature reached ninety degrees Les decided not to work. "I think I will stay in today Poppet (his pet name for me) and rest, I don't want to go out at all today." "Sure" I said "you have been over-doing things lately maybe I will leave you to rest and go into town and do some shopping." He gave me some money insisting that I take a taxi into the centre of Melbourne. He saw me off at the door still in his pyjamas and I remember the pyjama legs drooping concertinaed around his slippers. I had a good day shopping and chatting in the bars and it was around four thirty or five o'clock when I returned home. I went through the front door calling "Les I'm back where are you?"

There was no answering call and I assumed that he had gone out for a drink after all, but then I saw his cigarettes and lighter on the table in the sitting room and thought that I would take a look upstairs. There he was, lying in bed with the morning paper clasped in his upright hands.

"What are you doing up here so quiet, didn't you hear me call?"

There was no reply and then I realised just how still the room was and just how quiet Les was, I couldn't even hear him breathe. I pulled at the newspaper, it slipped out of his hands which stayed in position and then I saw that in spite of the heat he was cold when I touched him and his skin looked blue. Now I know that he had been dead for hours, but then I panicked – running next door to Pam, the Landlord's wife, calling out as I ran "Pam come quickly, something is wrong with Les, I need a doctor." Luckily we all used the same local doctor so she had the number and the doctor came quickly. The other tenants heard my shouting and gathered round wondering what had happened.

When the doctor came I shouted "Quick please help me Les is sick and you must do something." I hurried the doctor upstairs to Les but it didn't take him long to examine Les and tell me "Peter he is dead I'm sorry but I cannot do anything for him." I couldn't accept this and begged him "surely you can revive him, there must be something you can do." My head hurt and my heart was pounding so hard that I felt as if it would burst from my chest and I thought that I would die as well. Then other people came and gently helped me downstairs where the doctor gave me three tablets, I swallowed one immediately without waiting for water and someone, I don't know who, held me until I started to calm down a little.

"I have to call an Ambulance and the Police." said the doctor following on with his routine and I remembered that I also had to call someone, my priest Father Martin who had received me into the church. Father Martin answered his telephone and came very quickly, I took him upstairs where he gave Les absolution and then waited with me until the Police and Ambulance men came. They had great difficulty in carrying Les down the winding staircase, his body was rigid and the stair was narrow.

Father Martin and I went into the kitchen where we perched on the two kitchen stools. At first we just sat there with the sounds of the commotion going on outside and then we were suddenly alone in the house, I started to cry and Father Martin gave me his crisp fresh handkerchief to use. His face had such a compassionate look that I wanted to talk. Father please help me I don't know what to do." If you kneel down Peter I will give you my blessing." I knelt down and said "You do realise that I loved him?" "Yes Peter you were obviously good friends." "But Father, we were more than just friends, we were in love, what can I do now?"

I can't remember his exact words but they were full of comfort and love and with no condemnation which might have been expected in those days when a persons sexuality was not so easy to defend as it may be now.

I did try to contact Les' family in England to see if they had any wishes for the funeral arrangements but they showed no interest in the funeral or me. But of course later on they did send someone to see if he had left any money or insurance, so either I had to do something or it was a pauper's grave for Les and I couldn't let that happen.

We had attended a funeral recently and I went to the Funeral Directors in North Melbourne, near to the Victorian Market. I had no money but came to an arrangement to pay as soon as I could. It was a small funeral, about twelve people, Father Martin took the service and I had arranged for Les to be buried in the New Cheltenham Cemetery close to where our friend Millie was buried.

After the funeral I thought I would stay in Australia but as I had already written to my family telling them that I was coming home I couldn't disappoint them, especially my Mother who I knew would have been upset. I didn't tell them what had happened but Just that I would be home later in the year. We had been renting a two bedroom house that was part of a converted dairy and stables behind one of those imposing mansions that they used to build in Australia, near to the beach at Elwood.

It had been furnished with such care and love but I left it the same night that Les died and I didn't go back except to pack and arrange the sale of the furniture. I fancied I could hear him breathing in every room, the doctor had given me sedatives but I couldn't stay there and went to stay with Wally and his sister Dossie who lived opposite. I managed to sell the furniture to a newly arrived German man who was setting up house. But after I had paid for the funeral and put aside some money for my fare home there was nothing left and I had to pay Wally for my board and get some money to take to England with me. I hadn't worked in Australia and was a bit out of practice with job hunting. Dossie had some good ideas, she had a silk, low cut dress that she wore for interviews and kept a stock of headed notepaper that she used to write her own references on.

I took her advice and armed with a false C.V. and fake references tried to get work. Unfortunately the wool market was down and Australia was going through a bout of unemployment. Melbourne was full of people from other states looking for work and they were more experienced than I was. Eventually I ended up at the Tramways recruiting centre somewhere on Flinders Street Railway Station where I was interviewed by a kindly man who guided me through the intricacies of form filling and who seemed to think me most suitable for the job of conductor.

The Melbourne Tramways had a life all their own that you don't see as a passenger. We carried the money in big leather satchels along with our cigarettes and food, some of the women kept their knitting in the satchels and knitted as they passed along calling for fares. To say that the passengers were just a necessary evil is mild, we barely tolerated them. The whole purpose as we saw it, of the driver and conductor was to get from depot to terminal as quickly as possible, disregarding any timetable the Tramways Board had in mind. We raced along the track, rattling from side to side. Some drivers could actually coast through a stop, letting the agile passengers on but not quite coming to a halt. A quick pull on the bell rope by the conductor and it was like flying to the next stop. Woe betide any passenger that stumbled. "Please don't stand up until the tram stops, it isn't safe and I am responsible for you." The phrase was constantly on my lips and the chastened passenger alighted sure that they had in some way violated a sacred byelaw. I shouted quite a lot because I was afraid they might rightly blame me for ringing the bell too quickly.

One morning before I left for work a young policeman called at the house to tell me that the date had been set for Les' inquest, he told me that I would have to tell the Coroner how I had found Les and try to tell them what he had been like in the days before his death. The young policeman was very concerned when he realised just how upset I was by it all and offered to escort me on the day. I was very pleased with his attitude and also I had been pleased that the inquest had taken so long to happen. It meant that Les had been able to have a Catholic funeral without the question of suicide which had been on my mind even though I didn't mention that to anyone.

The Coroner said that the autopsy showed such a large amount of drugs in the stomach that it was impossible for there to have been an accident. Les had taken his own life. I didn't know why then and I have never been able to explain it satisfactorily to myself, probably it was just something in-built, a self destruct syndrome. In the bar of the Hotel Australia in Collins Street I met an Englishman who told me that he had known Les in London in the Thirties, they had first met at a party given for Jessie Matthews. "Les always had plenty of money even in those days" he told me "Les used to drive a red sports car and always had beautiful young men with him, but he drank far too much and was given to bouts of depression."

I knew that he drank heavily while I knew him but didn't know that it had been for so long. It seems strange to have lived with a person for three years and still know hardly anything about them. When I was going through his papers trying to find his family address in England I came across an old snapshot of a young man on a bicycle, on the back is a message 'A ce ami L.Roberts en souvenir de notre sejour au Lazarett De Marienburg – Flaubert 8-42 Prusse 02/9.' The words are written in pencil but in ink across the back is the date September 1938. The young man on the bicycle is wearing plus fours and looks very nice, I still have the snapshot and often study the young man as if he could somehow throw some light on the Les of long ago; I feel a nostalgia for what was, even though I was never there in Lazarett De Marienburg where they had their encounter. He looks out at me and perhaps I am looking at my own youth that has now gone no matter how much I pretend other-wise.

At first after Les died I would spend my free time mooning alone the beach re-tracing our old walks and wishing that Les could come back to me; but then gradually with the good help of Wally and his sister I started to go out to the bars and accept invitations to parties. I began to feel alive again and realised that I would not be alone forever as I had imagined during the first weeks of widowhood. A lot of very nice men worked on the Trams and one in particular paid a lot of attention to me, he was about 17 years old, very quiet and I thought at first from his accent that he had come from France but he was a Mauritian. He was so kind to me when we met but the first time he asked me to his apartment for a meal he confessed shyly to me that he could get an erection easily " But I don't cum, it just goes on and on, I am sure that something is wrong with me." "Don't worry about it," said Peter the instant Sex therapist, "I will help you."

We spent many nights trying to remedy his problem and during the days at work we exchanged many loving glances and waves as our trams passed each other on the way in and out of the city. But then his family came from Mauritius to join him, he went back to College and our romance was over and anyway I had saved the money I needed. I confirmed my booking and applied for my tax clearance which was necessary before my ticket could be issued and set sail for England.

The ship sailed at 11pm and that evening Wally, Dossie and an assortment of friends came on board to see me off, after several bottles of sherry it was quite a party.

When the time came for them to go ashore they waited on the edge of the dock for the ship to sail and threw streamers at me, the more streamers you can catch the better and all of us on board held on to them for as long as possible, keeping the contact with the shore and our friends. Slightly jingoistic tunes blared from the ship's loudspeakers and we were away.

CHAPTER TWO.

To save money I had taken a berth in a five berth cabin, the other four were all returning home disillusioned with Australia and couldn't understand how I could have liked being there so much; but then they didn't know that for most of the time I hadn't had to work and had been able to spend hours each day fishing at the end of the breakwater.

When I left England for Australia I only drank milk but when I left Australia for England I drank everything especially alcohol and the journey passed in a haze of duty free liquor. This time I went through the Great Australian Bight without a scratch, drinking on the top deck with Betty a doctor and Marina an interesting woman who was trying to create an impression of a wealthy independent traveller but whose accent veered sharply between Canadian, Australian, Standard English and most often Cockney.

Until we turned around Spain into the Atlantic the weather was superb, hot sunny days and the P & O food even in the tourist class was excellent. It took a good half hour to read the menu for each meal and probably the best part of an hour and a half to eat the food. Every day the kitchens turned out fresh bread and rolls and the selection of meats and fish seemed endless. The Goanese dining room staff liked me and showed it by their smiles and gifts of little luxuries from the first class menu, like the beautiful almond petit fours which I ate at night while lying on my bunk. As the journey progressed and I relaxed more I started to take an interest in some of the male passengers but my constant companion was Mario who was returning home to Rome. But that was a purely brotherly friendship, for sensual companionship it was hard to choose between the deck crew, my cabin steward and after Aden the Arab businessmen. I decided it was too hard to choose and as no one person captured my heart did my best to accommodate them all, especially the Arabs who were so gentle and excited by my white skin and this in turn excited me.

When the ship docked in Colombo, Mario and I went ashore together. We were soon accosted by a charming man who wanted to be our guide and show us the sights of Colombo. My first reaction was to say that I had no money but of course he had an answer for that. "But you are so nice, you don't need money, let me give you a present" said my new friend who then presented me with a large pearl pin.

Mario and I decided that we may as well go along with Ram, Colombo was so crowded, the streets were full of people and we had no idea where we should go by ourselves. Ram was delighted and hustled us along the streets trying to tempt us into the small shops where he obviously knew the owners but we resisted all his attempts until we came upon the Hotel Metropole and then it was me that suggested we went in there. Inside, away from the streets, it was a different Colombo, air conditioned splendour and handsome men in tailored suits. There I learnt the delights of a local drink called Arrack which is made from the coconut palm. This is a strong clear spirit with a special taste and I soon felt irresistible as alcohol can make you feel. Ram was not a drinking man and after about an hour he suggested to Mario that we should leave the bar and let him show us a bit more of Colombo. After considering all his options we decided that it might be nice to take a trip in one of the local buses to Mount Lavinia. The road wound along the coast through banana plantations and huge Frangipani trees with their fragrant pink flowers until we came to a small hotel where we alighted. The air was heavy with the scent of the Frangipani trees and we could see the coconut palms growing out from the Shore, leaning out over the ocean. We went to the bar of the hotel where we drank Tiger beer and the waiters flirted with me to the consternation of some of the lady passengers from the ship who had thought the attention would be solely directed at them. I didn't take any notice; I had never been in such a beautiful place, the tourist advertisements used to refer to Ceylon as a Pearl of an Island and it truly is.

Later on we travelled back down the long road back into Colombo and I thought it would be nice to buy something for a souvenir and Ram took Mario and I to a shop selling cloth, where the owner insisted on dressing me in a blue and gold sari. We stood outside the shop where the owner with his family and many of the other shopkeepers posed with me and took many pictures. They told me that I looked like a real Indian Prince, I wasn't sure that a Prince would wear a sari but let it pass as we were all having such a good time and I liked being flattered in such a charming way.

Declining to buy a sari both Mario and I (both drunk as lords) bought sarongs which the local men wore and with our trousers wrapped in neat parcels said goodbye to Ram and made our way back to the ship wearing our sarongs with pink frangipani flowers behind our ears. From the reception we received in the streets as we made our way back to the ship, wearing sarongs was the best compliment we could have made to the Colombo citizens who were more used to seeing Europeans from behind glass as they swooped around in their fast cars with no thought of the safety of the people in the crowded streets. The men all wanted to touch my shoulders and tell me how happy they were to see that I liked their custom of wearing sarongs.

Mario and I made quite a show when we staggered up the gangplank and I kept my sarong on through dinner and during the dancing that night whirled around the floor until I fell down and had to be escorted to my cabin by two of the new passengers, dark handsome young Singhalese on their way to study in London.

Two days later we were passing through the Suez Canal and a lot of the passengers went ashore at the start of the canal to tour the Pyramids but as I didn't have that much money I decided to stay on board until we reached

Port Said. When we did reach Port Said we couldn't go ashore until the evening and after one of those long P & O dinners and a bottle wine drunk alone I was in a very relaxed mood. We had to reach the shore across a sort of floating bridge which was clustered with men selling sweets and souvenirs and who all seemed to have extra hands with which to touch me. The noise and the shouting that followed my progress along this floating pathway filled the night air. First one man started calling out at me "Oh pretty blond boy, come and let me be your husband." Then another "Come home with me and I make you feel good, you never had it like me." Most often they just said "Touch me here Blondie, touch me here." The outlines of their cocks pushed through the cotton of their long shirts as they made their wishes doubly obvious in case I hadn't heard the words. This was my first experience of being Blond in a dark country and I loved it, as soon as I reached the shore I met up with Marina who's idea of a good time seemed to coincide with mine. "Oh my God Peter just look at those men, don't you just love this?" We walked along together and then allowed ourselves to be persuaded to go into a bar where we could see people dancing. We drank gin that tasted more like surgical spirits than Gilbeys but we didn't care. Marina, dancing around the floor with a handsome young man paused just long enough to say, "Let's jump ship and stay here forever." As I was sitting at a table with two charming men who were flirting outrageously I must admit that I thought it a good idea as well, but I didn't stay with her and some hours later found myself in the street in the company of three young men who treated me to soft drinks and sweetmeats and said that they wanted to take me to a museum. They all had bicycles and let me ride them and we played along the street like four schoolboys. Of course I was enchanted, excited and entirely drunk and when they suggested the museum I couldn't wait to get started. They assured me that I would really enjoy it and although the route to the museum soon led away from the lighted streets it didn't occur to me why or that it would be an unusual museum to be open in the middle of the night. That is until the two Singhalese men from the ship saw me and joined us. They persuaded the Egyptians to leave, one telling them "This boy is my wife, go away from him I am very jealous."

"But I'm going to see a museum" I protested, but they insisted and escorted me back to the ship exclaiming loudly at my foolishness.

The next morning when I woke, sober, I realised how lucky I had been. The British invasion of the Suez Canal had left a bad feeling with many people there and also a lot of the white people on the ships were very abusive towards the Egyptians.

The boys may just have wanted to have sex with me but they could just as well have meant harm. If the Singhalese hadn't intervened I may have ended up as a statistic, who can tell.

That was the last of my adventures ashore except for Naples where I was pursued ashore by members of the deck crew, all Northern lads with a taste for sex and red wine. We toured Naples in a haze of alcohol and quick sex, under bridges, in restaurant bathrooms and any convenient doorway they could push me into, arguing over whose turn it was next. They knew Naples very well and I didn't do any touristy sight seeing that day, nor did I see any of the other passengers from the ship or any of the cabin crew. In every walk of life it seems that there are sub-cultures and sub sub-cultures.

CHAPTER THREE.

After four weeks of being aboard ship with the sun shining every day and nothing to do but laze around, eat and drink it was a shock when we turned into the Channel and be greeted by the English fog. I began to wonder if I had done the right thing in coming to England, it might have been better if I had stayed put, saved more and then asked my family to join me in Australia instead of returning back to this. The passengers coming to Europe for the first time came down from the upper decks in a state of some shock with a look of disbelief on their faces, especially those from hot countries. One young woman from India asked me "What is that horrible stuff you can smell in the air?" "This is the famous London fog" I told her "But this is nothing, just wait until it is really cold and the fog swirls around your feet."

When we docked we came down the gangplank straight into the customs hall and it was definitely HOME, dull and dismal. Every bag and trunk was thoroughly turned over and searched. "What's this stuff then?" on seeing my bottles of Arrack carefully packed. "It's a local drink from Ceylon." "Is it like whisky?"

"Oh no, it's just a drink made from a tree" I tried to look as healthy as I could.

"Well I don't know what it is but I suppose it's alright." The Customs Officer made a chalk scrawl on my cases and then I was on the train to London.

I took a taxi to Streatham and a reunion with my family. On the way home the streets seemed to be disappointingly the same as when I had left them but it was 1961 and some things had changed during the three years that I had been away.

Australia kept one apart somehow from the rest of the world, if I had one criticism about Australia is was the remoteness from what was happening abroad. Maybe it was just me and I had insulated myself in my world of domestic bliss and hadn't taken any notice of all the things going on around me.

But of course things were moving. In Africa things were changing rapidly, the violence in the Congo had ceased but the first Prime Minister Lamumba had been exiled in Katanga and unrest was everywhere else but at least the Africans were realising freedom could come.

In England betting shops had been legalized since May and on the radio popular music played all day where before it had been confined to an hour on Sunday mornings and then a very broad mixture of music. Of course there had been Radio Luxembourg but that was difficult to hear and kept fading away all the time. My Mother was enthusiastic about a programme that had recently started on television called Coronation Street which she said "Everybody watches it because it is so realistic." My Stepfather just missed the old days before betting shops when the bookies runner would call daily, asking "Anything for me today?"

The personal touch had now gone from betting and big business and taxation had stepped in. At first I felt that I would never settle down again to the English way of living, the weather and the way people seemed satisfied with what I thought was second best service in the shops. But gradually as I relaxed and started to take more notice of the changes I realised that people were more prosperous than before, girls had adopted the fashion of wearing several rings on each hand where before they were lucky if they had both and engagement and wedding ring. In the shops the old one-ounce packets of butter and half-ounce packets of tea had been replaced by larger sizes and even the chocolate bars had increased in size from the two ounce bars to include even one pound weight bars; a far cry from the days I knew before I left for Australia when sweet rationing hadn't been over for very long.

One big change was the number of black people from the Caribbean. Every day more arrived and every day the debate on television and radio continued. There were predictions of catastrophe and chaos and on one occasion I heard a well meaning but confused person say "Of course we should be pleased that these people are coming to England, each one is a potential entertainer, they can all dance and sing." Not a word about their professional skills as teachers, doctors and engineers of their political awareness. The fact that they had been abandoned by the sugar barons who no longer needed their labour was not mentioned. But even now in the 1990's there is no broad appreciation of the assets people were bringing to our island when they landed in those cold bleak inhospitable winter days of 1961/2 and even in the 1950's. I have always been pleased that I had been present in the fifties to receive people at Waterloo and help them to find accommodation and settle. My family all agreed that it was a good thing. As a child at school I had been taught that the British Empire meant that we were all brothers and sisters whatever colour we were, we were all one people. This had impressed me as a child and I spent long hours searching in the mirror for some clue to an ancestry other than my immediate family.

My Grandmother from Skinningrove in Yorkshire had dark curly hair and deep brown eyes but all my uncles were blond as my Mother had been. I didn't know then what my Father or his family were like as we were what is now known euphemistically as a one parent family, that was until 1938 when my Mother married and I had a Father.

In our street was a family with three girls and one of them started to go out with a handsome black man who escorted her to and from the house with great style.

Her family met any criticism from their neighbours with great vigour who defended her right to do exactly as she pleased and see whomsoever she liked; that is until she started to produce black nephews for them. But life and romance are unstoppable and all over London pretty tanned babies started to appear. I felt so lucky that my family could not see the need to differentiate between skin colours, but the whole atmosphere lent spice to my Mother's shopping expeditions as she championed the right of black women to buy where they liked and take full part in the life of the community.

My Mother had bought me a new double bed for my room as she had assumed that I would be bringing Les home with me. She, in typical fashion, did not question me when I came home alone but after a day or so I explained that Les had died suddenly. I didn't go into details and she accepted this, being glad that I had come home and I suppose she thought that I would stay with her from now on. But just about ten days after I arrived back in England I met Vincent.

I had been to the cinema in Streatham and as it was a nice night I decided to walk home across Tooting Bec Common. He was waiting there as if he had come clear across the world just to meet me. "Do you have the time?" His opening remark was so clichéd that I laughed out loud but we soon began talking, I was hooked and so was he, he was wearing a camel hair overcoat and with his thick set body and wavy hair looked like a dark Arab. From that day we were together and not one day passed that didn't find us together at some point. On that first night we went back to his room in Ritherdon Road in Balham and we talked and made love and talked and made love again until it was daylight and he walked me home across the common. "Where are you from, which island?" I had asked him.

"I'm not from an island I'm from British Guiana in South America," he said proudly.

I had never heard of British Guiana, later after independence to be called Guyana, but in the years to follow I came to know more about British Guiana and the Guyanese than I ever did about England and the English.

We arranged to meet the next day so that I could take him home to meet my Mother.

In the morning I told my Mother that I had met someone that I thought I would spend my future with. "Again" she exclaimed, "I thought you would have enough of that by now and want to live your life for yourself." But of course she agreed to meet him, she had great understanding and love for me and although outwardly appearing somewhat strait-laced she was a loving passionate woman, caring of her family, especially me.

I was nervous of them meeting at first but both Vincent and my Mother were immediately enchanted with each other. I cooked omelettes for them and they ate and talked about me as if I were not there and as if they had known each other for a long time.

"I wonder how he will cope with the cold winter" my Mother asked me after he had left. "I don't know – I hadn't thought of that." Then I did start to think about it and almost missed when she said "He is very nice, I like him a lot, he reminds me of your Father" then she went on and said, "I wonder what Dad will think of him." If I had been listening properly I might have thought to ask her why she had differentiated between Father and Dad and gotten to know just who my Father had been.

We always assumed my Stepfather innocent of the sexual ways of the world and he usually showed no interest in my friends but he was more affectionate towards me than to his children by his previous marriage and even towards my half-brother, even though he had been jealous of me when he first married my Mother.

Dad accepted Vincent easily and encouraged me in

the friendship. Their acceptance of Vincent and later Vincent's family with their ready acceptance of me was a good basis for our long if somewhat stormy relationship.

At the time Vincent was living in Ritherdon Road which was just across the common from my Mothers house and I saw him every day. He was at Tooting Bec Hospital "Studying psychiatry" was how he put it, but he left after "They wanted me to do cleaning and not studying." I was shocked and enlisted the help of the newly formed Campaign Against Racial Discrimination C.A.R.D. but Vincent wasn't keen to force the issue so we dropped it. I later found out that he had been a student nurse and left the first day he was asked to change a bedpan, so much for psychiatry. This was my first experience of Vincent's cavalier attitude to authority and truthfulness, which should have alerted me to what was to follow but my mind excused any doubts that I might have had; being so besotted with his strength and vigour and the sexual prowess that was a new experience for me.

The C.A.R.D. soon gained enormous popularity amongst the native white people especially the more thinking and articulate of us. Sadly some black people resented what they saw as a colonial attitude and the campaign was abandoned to be taken up later as a political issue by black people themselves.

I started to look for work but as the only employment I'd had in the past three years was on Melbourne Tramways it didn't seem to fit in with anything clerical and I wasn't having much luck. Before I went to Australia I had worked for the US Air Force in Grosvenor Square and when I went to visit them the Colonel offered me a position. They were glad to have me back there but I didn't settle down well, all I could think of was Vincent and of when I would see him next.

My immediate supervisor, a civilian came from Italy via the Congo where he had been accustomed to an easy colonial life, we didn't get on at all and I resented his attitude towards anyone of colour. When Vincent made his usual daily call, the supervisor always seemed to answer the telephone – handing it to me with a scowl and a reminder that I hadn't yet finished my work.

Although I started work at 8.30 each morning I was with Vincent every night until two in the morning and then I was edgy during the day until he called me.

One day the Colonel gave a party at work. I can't remember the reason they were celebrating, there were so many occasions and holidays that were given.

They celebrated the English holidays, the North American holidays and most of the holidays that were celebrated in the countries where the U.S. had bases. I was so tired that day and decided to take a couple of those small tablets that Les had given to me. At first they seemed to perk me up but during the party I started flagging and thought I hadn't taken enough of them. I took four more and that was the last thing I remembered. I blacked out until the next morning when I woke up in Vincent's bed. This was the first complete night I had spent there and I didn't know anything about it. I had been taken there by a colleague who had been asked to take me home after I collapsed at work, they thought it was just the alcohol, they didn't know about the pills. When my escort tried to get directions from me I kept calling "Vincent, Vincent, I must go to Vincent" and insisted that he take me to Ritherdon Road. Vincent had been delighted by the fact that I had stayed, he didn't mind in what condition as long as I was dependent on him.

After the pills and alcohol I felt very shaky for what seemed like weeks and my job being very boring didn't help, at times my heart seemed to pound too strongly and I felt weak and without any energy. One morning while I was walking down the stairs in the office building I felt as if I was about to faint and fall. The Colonel's secretary, Joan, saw me and helped me into the Colonel's office where she broke an amyl ampoule under my nose. This brought me around quickly and Joan put me in a taxi so that I could go home. The taxi had just started to go down Park Lane when I felt that everything was getting dim and I couldn't breath properly. I was convinced that my heart was stopping. "Quick, quick, go to a hospital, I am dying."

I had enough breath to shout. The taxi driver took me to St. Georges Hospital at Hyde Park where I rushed in calling "Help me please help me I am dying." I was in such obvious distress that I wasn't kept waiting but after a thorough examination, during which I panicked and jerked my arms and legs about, the Outpatient Doctor told me "It's just an anxiety attack, please try to relax, breathe deeply, take these tablets." I took the tablets just to please him as I was sure they wouldn't work but after a while I did begin to feel calmer and my heart stopped pounding so much and I decided that I could continue my journey home. The tablets did work to a degree, actually they were just a larger dose of the phenobarbitone that I had already used.

My heart periodically pounded and I couldn't concentrate enough to work. I had time off sick and spent the days just waiting to see Vincent. It was impossible for me to see enough of Vincent. While I had been at work I would leave the train at Balham instead of Streatham Common so that I could pass by his house to have a quick visit before going home to eat and get ready to come out again to see him. Those quick visits were not really a good idea, his room was always full with people, men talking or women having their done. Vincent was good at pressing hair with hot combs and styling it with what looked to me like old-fashioned curling tongs and he also seemed to know everything that went on in the Guyanese community around Balham, it was a good place to go to learn the latest gossip. Consequently I didn't see him alone during the day unless I came home from work early and we sneaked in so that no-one would know he was at home. During the evenings too he had many callers and it was usually very late when we were able to be alone and go to bed together for one or two hours. Each morning came too quickly and every day had been a struggle to get to work.

Our street in Streatham was on the route to the local cemetery and every morning I saw the hearses pass which in my condition did nothing to make me feel better.

Dad suggested that to take my mind off things I might like to help him paint the house. I thought yes it might be good therapy for me and keep my mind occupied during the day when I wasn't seeing Vincent. We decided to do the job properly, Dad was working at a paint factory and he bought home some red lead to paint over the cracks, quality undercoat and topcoat. I started out doing it really well, like an old time professional, but before I had finished we decided to sell the house and I finished it off by filling in the cracks with polyfilla and just giving the back of the house one coat of thickly applied topcoat. Before I worked for the U.S. Air force I had worked for a builder and I knew how to make things look good without making too much effort.

My brother, Alan, had recently met a girl from Yorkshire, like me he brought his new friend straight home to meet Mother. He was head over heels in love and talked of going up to Yorkshire to live, my Mother had been born in Skinningrove near Saltburn and my sister still lived in Loftus, which is the next village. House prices in the North were much lower than in London and we still had a small mortgage to pay. "You could buy a house in Yorkshire without a mortgage and still have some money to spend" I reasoned with my Mother. Dad was about to retire and my Mother was going through an anxiety state similar to mine so she welcomed the thought of getting away from London to a quieter environment.

Mum and Dad arranged to go to Bradford and stay with the family of Alan's girlfriend so that they could look around for a suitable house that we could afford.

They found a house very quickly in Shipley that they both liked. The house was an old back-to-back house made of local stone with even a stone staircase, no problem of dry rot there unlike the house in Streatham which was riddled with dry rot caused by my Mother making her own D.I.Y. repairs with pieces of old wood she found in the garden. Although the house in Shipley had no back garden the front garden was quite large, full of rose bushes and the neighbours were friendly. Mum and Dad were both ready for a change, Dad had never been one to make friends readily, when he wasn't working he just sat indoor with no interest in what went on outside the house.

In Yorkshire they both found life was much easier and they had the independence of no mortgage and with some money to spend had a freedom they had not had before.

Dad spent many hours in the garden pottering around and talking to the neighbours while Mother soon settled back into her Yorkshire roots.

Vincent was now signing on at the Employment Exchange and in those days you had to go for any job they had available, like it or not, or otherwise lose benefits.

He was sent to work as a labourer in a bottle yard somewhere in Streatham Vale and then it was his turn to pass my house twice a day. By this time I was so tired and on edge all the time and I felt the reaction for the first time from Les' death.

The process of death in the white community leaves everything bottled up, no-one talks about the dead person and the funeral is very functional so unlike the Caribbean and Irish way where one is encouraged to show plenty of emotion at funerals and to talk about the person that has died. I had everything squeezed up inside me waiting to explode. Being on sick leave from the Americans I was able to be at home when Vincent called, my parents being in Yorkshire so apart from my brother who was working we had the house to ourselves. After the first day at his new work Vincent came straight home to me each night and I would cook for him and he was able to stay with me all night – leaving for work in the morning just before my brother got up. Away from the environment of Balham with so many people around we were able to make love more freely and frequently and relaxed completely with each other.

One evening on the way back from the bottle yard Vincent collected a large bunch of privet from a garden hedge and that night when he had already made love to me several times and I had reached a state of high excitement he started to beat me with the branches, which he held like a birch broom. I didn't know that it could be so pleasurable to be beaten. I moved about the bed indulging myself in pure feelings of enjoyment as he beat me without saying a word, just holding his tongue in his cheek and making guttural noises. When he stopped beating and entered me again it was like stars exploding. The experience released my spirit as it had never been released before and after that Vincent frequently used some form of sadism in our Lovemaking and I encouraged him. Sometimes my body would be bruised and yellow from the deep bites he made. Vincent knew just how to arouse me, he told me tales of his youth when his friends would have sex with their pet dogs and of the Asian merchants who encouraged the young boys to have sex with them when their parents sent them to buy groceries. The way he used my body as an endless source of pleasure for himself and the words he used and the stories he told me while he entered me over and over kept me in a continuous state of excitement and just the touch of him made my body open up to him without any reservation. This was the first time I had met a man who could make love more than once in an evening, well maybe there had been one or two that could manage a couple of times after a long period of rest, but Vincent would perform over and over again without any break.

When my parents decided to move to Yorkshire, Vincent and I knew that we would live together.

CHAPTER FOUR.

In 1962 it wasn't so common for black and white people to live together but we weren't interested in what anyone thought and in any case both our families approved of our friendship so we were confident that we would be all right.

Vincent had one cousin a mature lady known as Aunt Carrie with a wicked sense of humour. One morning she and I were walking in Balham together when she suddenly turned to me and said "Quick, hug me up Peter and kiss me – someone is staring at you walking with this old black woman." We kissed and laughed at the foolishness of the whole thing, but from then we made a big show of kissing in public as if to make a statement of our friendship and the way we felt about prejudice.

Aunt Carrie was living on the ground floor of a large house in Balham with her eldest daughter. During the day she looked after an assortment of grand and great Grandchildren, the landlord was from Guyana and both he and his wife like Vincent and I. They rented us the top half of the house, above Aunt Carrie and we all lived like one big family. Aunt Carrie's younger daughter Ruth lived in Ritherdon Road near to where Vincent had first stayed. Ruth was a childrens nurse and she could cook brilliantly as well, Ruth and I took to each other immediately.

Vincent also had a reputation for being a good cook and as we had no facilities for cooking in quantities he was always calling on Ruth for help, whenever he took orders for meat patties or cakes Ruth was the one who made them. When Vincent's customers came to collect their orders he made sure to let them know that he had just taken them out of the oven himself, taking all the credit and not mentioning Ruth at all. Ruth's only son Clem became my special friend and spent many days with me, helping me to shop and watching me cook and on Saturdays we went to the cinema in the afternoon and afterwards went home to cook, Clem didn't mind what we cooked as long as crinkly chips were included.

One morning we were walking along Balham High Road, Clem's little hand firmly clasped in mine as usual, when he asked me "Uncle Peter, do you think you could give me a penny?" I asked him why only a penny as even in those days there was not much that a penny could buy. He replied, "I only need a penny then I can buy this thing from Woolworth's." "Okay Clem, let's go into Woolworth's and you can show me what you want to buy." When we got to Woolworth's the desired 'thing' was as always a gift for his mother Ruth and cost about two shillings and sixpence. "If I give you a penny will you have that much Clem?" He calculated in his mind and said "Well Uncle Peter, if you give me the penny then

I will ask mummy for the three I have saved and then I will get some more from Uncle Gil."

In his mind he had it worked out so well, we bought the present together and he beamed with pleasure quite convinced that all he had needed was that one-penny.

By now the U.S. Air force had grown tired of my sick leave and I had to leave them.

The Colonel suggested that I had been overdoing the sick leave scenario as I had only been back working for them for less than a year and had more than a years equivalent of sick pay and holiday pay as well. He was worried that it would be difficult to justify this to the Air Force. What else could I do but resign gracefully thanking him for his understanding. I didn't want to stay there anyway, when I did go to work I was continually involved more and more in arguments involving racial prejudice that was prevalent there. I just couldn't understand how one of the woman, a staunch Catholic, could have such prejudices against black people not even wanting them to attend the same church as she did "They have their own churches" she said, "They can go there."

Vincent's job at the bottle yard hadn't lasted long so now both of us were signing on at the Labour Exchange. It was a bitterly cold winter and the queues at the Labour Exchange were long and slow moving. Many of the men were spending their first winter in this climate and it was the worst winter for years. It was a common sight to see the stripes of pyjamas flapping from beneath their trouser legs.

There was no money to buy the traditional long woollen underwear to use as a defence against the cold so instead they used the next best thing and kept their pyjamas on underneath their street clothes. The houses too were cold, in those days central heating was only for the well off and carpet meant just a large square in the middle of the sitting room and if you were lucky a small piece of old carpet beside the bed so that your feet didn't hit the cold lino when you got up in the morning.

For most of us central heating was still just a distant dream and the cost of burning an electric or gas heater was prohibitive especially when you had to insert coins into a meter and the landlord had adjusted the tariff to his advantage. Twice a week the paraffin man called around the streets, the blue or pink coloured paraffin was reputed to burn without much smell but all of us that had to use paraffin heaters were known from the smell that lingered on our clothes and in our hair. It kept us warm but at the cost of some lives as children were left alone with the heaters burning and often turned them over with the consequent burning down of the house.

Of course these were mostly new immigrants and that meant the authorities didn't worry as much as they might have done.

In that winter there were very few jobs available and I accompanied Vincent and other Caribbeans around the factories in Mitcham and Colliers Wood looking for work. It was an extremely hard task. Scarcely any vacancies but everywhere the signs saying, no Coloured – no Irish or European only, filled me with shame and disgust. After some forceful prompting from the Labour Exchange I applied for a course in Glass Blowing. I was sent to an adult training school at Waddon in Surrey and at first thought it might be a good idea, making friends with a lot of the other students including a woman who was going through the same sort of anxiety attacks that I was. This made me a little uneasy but I persisted with the initial induction training but as soon as I started on the practical work I knew it was the wrong thing for me. All I managed was to burn my hands and make a mess with the glass, it wasn't the fault of the instructor who was so patient with me, it was just that although I might look what people call artistic I'm not and just couldn't get the hang of it.

I didn't know how to get out of the course without being put off benefits so I went to my doctor and told him that glass blowing was making me more nervous. He agreed with me saying that I wasn't the type of person to do a job like that. He gave me a letter to take to the Labour Exchange saying that glass blowing was not suitable and that I shouldn't do it. Fortunately the Labour Exchange accepted this and not only Was I able to resume collecting benefit but I somehow got myself onto the disabled register, which meant that there were very few jobs they could send me for.

This was all very well but living was expensive and we could hardly manage on the money we got between us. "Vincent, we can't go on like this we must think of something, we can't keep signing on forever." "I know Peter and I don't want you to do anything else like that glass blowing, it's no good. I tell you what Peter why don't we do some hairdressing." It sounded good but I asked him just how we would go about it. He was full of ideas, he had obviously been thinking about it before. "We can divide up the front room with a curtain, get a hairdryer from one of the catalogues and put some cards in the shop window."

I could see this as being a way out of the no coloured work situation for Vincent and a way out of going to work each day for me. I bought a hairdryer from the catalogue, it was one that screwed onto the back of a chair but we thought it looked very professional. The curtains came from the catalogue as well and Vincent had brought hairdressing tools with him when he came to London. I wrote out some postcards to put in the newsagents windows and we started.

Vincent showed me how to press curly African hair. That is a process to straighten the hair with a brass comb, heating the comb on a paraffin stove and then holding the hair and pulling the hot comb through to produce the desired straight hair. Nowadays the use of chemicals predominates, the same sort of chemicals that are used to curl European hair are used to relax African hair so that it can be styled easily. Burnt fingers were the order of the day and the women expected to get small burns on the scalp and unlike the English hairdressers we had no mirrors for them to see just how much hair came away in the combs which we quickly hid, pressing hair was supposed to help it grow so we couldn't let them see just how much hair they lost each time they had their hair pressed. After the pressing comb came the marcel iron to curl the hair in large curls in the style of the day. The desire in the 60's was to look as European as possible – unfortunately. Skin bleaching creams were widely used by both women and men. They contained the same chemical used by European women to bleach out the liver spots that come on their hands at a certain age. Thankfully these creams are no longer so popular as they were dangerous to use.

As well as pressing hair we started to make our own hair dressing from a basis of petroleum jelly with various oils and chemicals including cantharides and bay rum which had the reputation of making hair grow, we used jasmine oil for perfume.

After much thought we decided to call it 'Wild Coconut Preparation'. I bought a few gross of opaque cream jars and had labels made at a printers in Streatham. I was excited when we finally got the labels, pale mauve with a coconut palm as the emblem. Not reckoning with Vincent's lack of staying power for business or work I thought that we would make a fortune and put advertisements for the hair dressing in all the Caribbean magazines and left samples all over London with chemists and hairdressers. But unfortunately Vincent's one staying power was for sex and that always made me forget or postpone things that I should have done. How could I know that since he left school he had been accustomed to making a much easier living, I was to learn about that later on.

At first I tried very hard with our Wild Coconut and after approaching the chemist shops and hairdressers managed to sell some, but only three or six jars at a time.

There were so many other products available and the manufacturers being much bigger that us could spend money on promotion that we couldn't, also the idea of special preparations for black people was a new concept in England.

One Sunday I went into Brixton with another Guyanese man, Coppel, and we went to every house in Railton Road. It took us all day, each house had four or six families and they all invited us in to talk, listen to music, have a drink and some even bought my hair dressing. It was while we were trying to sell hair dressing that Sunday that I learnt how to make a punch with Stout, Eggs, Condensed Milk and Vegetable Juice; all whisked up with chopped ice – what a delicious concoction.

"Good for the back" is how one man described it. The Back being a euphemism for a mans sexual ability. It was an enjoyable day but not a commercial success.

I soon realised that without considerable money spent on advertising it would be difficult to promote the hair dressing and Vincent had lost interest in the product as soon as it was made. Even though he knew how good it was he had no interest in the selling of it. I had always been a great believer in the stories that start – they only had £10 when they started and now they are millionaires – but I began to realise that although they probably did only have £10, somewhere in the background there was always a relative with considerable money and influence.

CHAPTER FIVE.

Sometimes Vincent and I walked for old times sake across the common where we had first met, we noticed the activities of the prostitutes on Bedford Hill and later that night Vincent had a proposal. "You know Peter, that couple that have just bought that large house in Ritherdon Road? Well I heard they got the money by the wife working part time at the same thing." I hadn't heard about this and asked him if he was sure. "Yes Peter, everybody in Balham knows about it, they are all saying that they don't know how the husband could have let his wife do it; but she is probably like you, you like sex so much it would even be easy for you." I had to think about it and asked him if it was possible for men to pay other men for sex.

"Just shows what you know, of course they do, it's common all over the world and if you had someone like me to arrange it, it would be easy." "But I don't want to get sick and anyway you wouldn't really like it." I told him, but he had it all worked out already. "It wouldn't be for long, just until we get the deposit for a house of our own and don't forget that I was a nurse in British Guiana for a long time, I can examine you and give you injections if you needed them; I can always get penicillin from one of those nurse girls in the hospital and before you have sex with a man make sure you squeeze the top of his cock and if it hurts him it probably means he is not well and then you don't do anything with him."

Later that night in bed we talked about it again, the talk excited him, excited us both, we started to count the number of times he fucked. "Seven times, then eight" I counted "Vincent if that had been eight different men how much would we have got?" He said he thought about twenty or thirty pounds, that was at least double what I would have expected to earn at a normal 9-5 job in a whole week and there was suddenly the possibility to make that much in just one night. Apart from the financial aspect it was most exciting even just to think about it and he was right I did enjoy sex more than anything else in the world. Vincent knew me very well and often said "I would trust Peter in a room with a million pounds but I wouldn't trust him with one man."

Vincent finally persuaded me that we should give it a try and I knew that I would be safe as long as he was around to look after me. At that time he was very strong and looked strong, solid and tough looking. The first night we waited until it was dark and left the house quietly so that no-one would know we were out of the house; at first we just went around the Bedford Hill area and the roads leading across the common. In the streets Vincent would approach the cars that slowed down and make all the arrangements with the men that wanted sex. After a while we toured the Somerleyton Road clubs where illegal drinking and dancing went on all night and had some successful nights there.

Gradually it became known among the men what was happening and some of the men we knew would come to the house during the day on the pretext of arranging a hairdo for their wife or a birthday cake and slip into the bedroom with me. This was the most secret of all, most of them were married and it would have been disastrous for them if their little vice had become public knowledge. For a while this was all successful, we were young, full of vigour and the encounter with strangers made our own sex life even more vigorous.

Vincent would enter me over and over for hours after we came home. It was as if he was trying to expunge the others from me and to establish his control over me, I had to tell him over and over that the others gave me no pleasure at all. "Of course they don't make me feel nice," I would say, "they are only business, you are the only one that makes me feel good."

But gradually he became more and more possessive and jealous and watched me all the time and made me account for each hour, even when I was shopping I had to be careful and not talk to anyone he didn't know.

Then he decided that no matter how lucrative at might be, he disliked the thought of someone else touching me; this was in spite of the fact that we hadn't yet accumulated enough money for deposit on a house but he said that if I decided to go off with one of the men that I met he would kill himself. I protested that of course I wouldn't but at the same time I was glad to stop. I realised just how risky the whole thing was and I had seen the faces of some of the women on Bedford Hill and I didn't want to end up looking like them with hard sad faces.

Although Vincent was jealous he was also a show off with his friends where I was concerned. He liked to show that he could control me and I must admit that he did. One of his old school friends came to visit and spend the day with us, he had nowhere to stay and that night slept on a large chair in our bedroom.

Knowing he was there at night did not stop Vincent from his usual performance and performance it was, this way and that way for hours, even more than usual and I who had been cold with sex before I had been awakened by Vincent could now continue having sex for as long as he could. The more I could take the more he could give, it was a Round Robin of lust.

We had neglected the hairdressing business for too long and as Vincent made the ladies wait a long time when they came most of our clients started to stay away and soon we only had about three regular clients.

One sunny morning an importer friend came to visit us with his new girl friend.

She was a very nervous woman who hand was clutched hard onto the strap of her handbag. When I looked questioningly at her hand she said that she was unable to undo her hand, I asked her why and she said that "My hand contracted and there is nothing that can be done unless I get an injection from the doctor." I hadn't heard anything like that before but it did seem possible I supposed. We all spent the day drinking and Robbie went out to buy food for Vincent to cook, the time passed by quickly and they asked us if they could stay and spend the night on the settee in the sitting room.

In the morning I saw that the hand had miraculously unclasped, maybe it was the company! After we had eaten some breakfast she said that she understood that we were very good hairdressers. I admitted that we did do hair and she asked if we could wash and set her hair. Vincent wasn't interested to do it but I thought we might as well take her money. As I had no experience of European hair I asked Vincent what I should do. "Just do the best you can," he said, "Just screw it up at the back and use plenty of hairpins." At least she hadn't asked for her hair to be cut, that was one of the good things about working with hard curly hair – it needed more encouragement to grow than cutting.

I took her into the kitchen to wash her hair, she had that long fly-away hair and it felt very soft and clingy unlike the nice short hair that I was accustomed to.

Still it wasn't too bad and I soon had her underneath the dryer. When her hair was dry I brushed it back from her face and got the back into some kind of a plait, then I twisted it around and managed to get it flat to the back of her head; I put in so many hairpins it was nearly solid with metal. "There," I said, "A lovely French pleat, it really suits you." She asked Robbie "How do I look?"

"Yes I think it's very nice," said Robbie, "I told you that Peter was good."

He hardly looked at the woman, he was anxious to leave and would have said anything, one night with her clutched hand had been enough for him and we never saw them together again.

Robbie, the importer, was a man ahead of his time, what became known in the 80's as a Thatcherite Entrepeneur. He would buy and sell anything, he imported brass pressing combs from Germany, cosmetics from the USA and Canada. I sometimes helped him by typing letters to suppliers abroad, he would assure them that he was supplying the whole of the U.K. with whatever they sold. He did this so convincingly that they would often give him unlimited credit, but only once, after selling the merchandise and using the money he would have to approach another supplier in another town. Some suppliers were a little more careful and only sent the goods on a strictly cash basis and then he would raise capital by taking on a partner. Somehow the new partner would get to pay for the goods and then when they went to the docks to clear the goods through Customs the unsuspecting partner would be left waiting at one entrance while Robbie excited through another. By the time the hapless partner realised what had happened Robbie had sold the goods on and was preparing for his next business deal. This course of action necessitated the regular disappearance of Robbie from Balham and then when things had quietened down and the partners blood pressure had presumably gone back to normal Robbie would re-appear always totally amazed at the reaction to what had been, according to him, a minor misunderstanding on the part of the other man, who "Should have waited for me, anyway I will settle it all when I get through with the business in Birmingham (or Manchester or Leicester)." Robbie was the perennial optimist, a clever and resourceful man and if the political climate had been different and he had been able to raise capital he could have done great things.

But this was in the 60's and black people were an unknown quantity to the Bankers and we didn't have the supporting policies of the GLC and local government as we did in the 70's and mostly in the 80's. But even now in the 90's it is still more difficult for a black person to start in business than a white or asian.

Hairdressing and prostitution had not proved to be the answer to our money situation.

While not abandoning everything altogether we branched out into the entertainment field. Vincent suggested that we should sell drinks at home, I said, "What do you mean sell drinks?" He said "Sit down and I'll tell you, in Guiana some people sell drinks from their home and also give parties and picnics where guests pay for drinks and food." He went on to explain how some people in Guiana made their living by selling various things from home. "Some women make black pudding which is very popular and then when their customers come to buy, usually at the weekend, they sell drinks to them as well or you can make bread and cakes and sell that, but drinks are the easiest and make the most money." There is an institution in Australia called 'Sly Grog' where it is possible to obtain alcohol after hours and I knew how popular it was there and thought that it was a good idea for us to try. The ever knowledgeable Robbie showed Vincent how to apply and get a Beer Sellers Licence. This was quite easy to get by paying £5 to the Customs Officer and agreeing to put a sign on the room that was to be used for storage. The licence enabled the holder to go direct to the breweries and buy beers at wholesale prices. In those days beer was all bottled, cans didn't arrive until later on when for weeks until we all got used to them we regularly sprayed beer over the walls and ourselves, the cans seemed to explode at a touch. We invested in bottles of Stingo, Guinness and various other lagers and as we didn't have any refrigeration we stacked the bottles inside a bath filled with cold water, the labels all soaked off but we managed.

This was much better than hairdressing, it was easier to handle and more people were interested in drinking than hairdressing especially as at that time the Caribbean Community was closer knit and hadn't started to expand into the native way of pubs and discos. As well as beer, a popular drink was Tarragona wine – whisky was too expensive for us to invest in and we sold the Tarragona wine by the bottle.

"Always give them large glasses," said Vincent, "That way they will drink it faster and buy another bottle and always put a glass out for yourself." I enjoyed this, it was very sociable, we had lots of friends who were nurses and we encouraged them to pop in when they were off duty. This helped the men to empty the bottles much quicker and with women around they wanted to spend more. The men who came to us for drinks made their own livings in many different ways, one man lived with a pretty girl who did limbo dancing and a little prostitution as well. To keep herself bright and awake through the long nights of her work she used to take some kind of drug.

Sometimes she came to meet her man in our flat, if she had been working she would come along the road with her face grey with fatigue and her feet dragging along the pavement. Once inside she would have a drink and take a couple of tablets from her purse and swallow them, after only minutes she would perk up, the colour would come back to her cheeks and she would chat and laugh and be ready to stay up until dawn. The sight of that girl with her grey face dragging along the road made me determined more than ever that I wouldn't use drugs, the experience with the phenobarbitone had also taught me how dangerous it could be. Apart from the 70's when Valium was a very popular prescribed drug I have resisted any blandishments to "Just try once," I am sure it is not worth the pain it leads to, even the universal marijuana, supposedly non-addictive, seems to have a lowering effect after a while.

Selling drinks proved much more popular than hairdressing and we soon had a score of regulars who came each day, bring their friends and we soon felt that we needed more space so that we could expand and hold the big parties that black people were accustomed to going to at weekends all over London then. Now the youngsters call the 'Blues' and think they invented them but in those days we just called them parties and got on with it. We decided to see if we could rent a larger flat where this would be possible. I had a friend called Michael from Yorkshire, he said that he was sharing a large flat in Wandsworth Common with four other boys but that they couldn't keep up with the rent and wanted to leave. They had to find someone to take over the tenancy before they could leave so Vincent and I went to look at the flat. "It is too expensive for us to keep on," said John a redheaded boy from the Midlands who seemed to be the only one of them actually working. "The trouble is that Alec had the tenancy and we all paid him our share of the rent but he hasn't been paying the landlord so we are in trouble." Alec was one of those well spoken hustler types, very impressive until it came to paying for anything himself.

The flat was just what we wanted with huge rooms, we decided we would try and get the tenancy. "Call the man Peter and you can tell him we are in business and then we will ask Robbie to give us a reference." Vincent was always quick with ideas like that. When we saw the landlord it was surprisingly easy, I suppose he thought at last he would get some rent for the flat because it was too big for most people at a rental of £12 a week when there were plenty of places going for £5.

Robbie agreed to furnish us with a reference and I went to his flat to type it out for him.

This was the time of Profumo, Christine Keller, Stephen Ward and the black boyfriend of Christine's 'Lucky Gordon'. Our way of life was beginning to seem to our friends as being like that, the only difference was that they were at the top of the social scene and we were down at the bottom. Nevertheless the comparison gave us a sort of cache amongst the drinkers and partygoers that moved around us especially when they saw the huge apartment that we had acquired. It was beautiful there, the lounge windows opened up onto an enormous garden and was large enough to accommodate three settees and still have room to hold a ball in. Almost every weekend we held a party and we had three spare bedrooms for what we euphemistically called 'Bed and Breakfast'.

There were a large number of men and women in our circle who were having affairs (some of the men a lot of affairs) and they always needed somewhere to go to be alone with is a very difficult thing when most of us lived in shared houses in a community that notices and comments on everything that you do. They felt safe coming to us as there were always so many people coming and going for different reasons, the women could say they came to have their hair done and the men could just say they went to Vincent's for a drink.

The bedrooms were in use most days with these couples who could just buy a bottle from Vincent and disappear for a few hours, or sometimes they would stay the whole weekend. Vincent was so good at arranging things like that and they knew they could rely on us to be discreet, which we were. Often the wife or husband of one of the couples would call for some reason and spend a pleasant afternoon with us completely unaware that their partner was also on the premises and in bed with someone else. I had to do a lot of talking on these occasions especially when the secret couple left by the front door while the unsuspecting partner was just a few feet away. But I enjoyed the excitement of this and Vincent just behaved as if this was what he had always done.

Robbie acquired yet another partner, but this time a Guyanese man who was more astute and even more devious than he was. He capitalized on Robbie's efforts and had gone legitimate by marrying the daughter of a bank manager and obtaining some capital so that he could set up business in Wardour Street as an Importer and Exporter. Soon after we moved into the Wandsworth Common flat this partner, Rogers, had started importing Danish lager in a big way and we soon had a hundred cases of lager stored in our cellar. We used this lager to supply our house parties which were very popular, every Saturday was a birthday for someone, we celebrated any and every occasion. 'Peter's birthday' Vincent's birthday' and as the countries of the Caribbean became independent we celebrated those. When Jamaica became independent in August 1962 we celebrated that with a splash. That was the night that we had our closest brush with the law so far. For our parties we usually played music on the record player which I had rigged up with two external speakers which were quite loud and sufficient for the purpose, but to especially mark the Jamaican independence party we decided to have one of the new sound systems that had become available. The men moved in with four huge speakers and lots of equipment and that night the music was very loud. In the height of the party two policemen appeared at the front door where I was standing. Hiding my panic I said, "Good evening officers, what do you want?" The officer standing nearest to me said "Sorry to bother you but we have had some complaints about the noise, what's going on in there?" I couldn't tell them about Jamaican Independence, they might have wanted to come in and see and then they would have seen Vincent at the bar selling drinks. "It's my Twenty-first birthday sir," I said smiling and I hoped innocently, "Why are they complaining?" He said that they had received complaints from two streets away and wondered what I was playing the music on. "It's just the radiogram, I'll go and turn it down"

I said, mentally crossing my fingers. Luckily inside news of the callers had spread and the music was turned down a little as they waited to see what would happen. For some reason the policemen were quite friendly towards me and didn't seem anxious to come past the front door thank God. "If you keep it turned down it will be all right," said the nice officer, "Happy birthday to you and goodnight."

I had always known that it would be a good policy for me to be at the door where my part was to admit guests who had to pay an entrance fee of 2/6 – no money – no entry – I even took stamps and Postal Orders. Inside a hundred and fifty mostly black people danced and drank but to any enquiry it was always "My birthday sir."

Whenever I see a film about the American prohibition memories of those exciting days come back and I feel nostalgic for them and remember all the fun we had.

Those were very happy days for Vincent and I, we had money! After everyone had left, usually around 4am in the morning, Vincent and I would count the money out into separate piles. "That's for the rent, that's for the electricity and gas and that's for us to spend." Vincent loved to sort out the money, in one night we could make enough to pay all our outgoings for the month. We were very relaxed then and would make love all day. Vincent moving up behind me when I was in the middle of washing up or cooking, whispering honeyed words as I think only a Guyanese man can. We made love in all the rooms, we made love on the floors and on the chairs, we made love standing up, sitting down, in every way our imagination could suggest. Vincent was so strong sexually and even after having sex all day would awaken me several times throughout the night and when we woke up in the mornings he had renewed energy and made love to me almost before I had properly awoken.

CHAPTER SIX.

Rogers the importer asked me if I would go to work for him in Wardour Street as his secretary. His wife was very jealous and was against him employing a woman but she approved of him employing me. She knew how much in love I was with Vincent and felt she could trust me and told Rogers to offer me the job.

As soon as I started to work there I realised even more just why she was jealous.

There was a filing cabinet in the office full of letters, passionate letters, from every kind of woman, young, old, single and married and all swearing undying love and support for this wonderful man, a lot of them referring to money they had given to him, some offering more money. Rogers was tall and handsome, not unlike Belafonte and with a charming carefree manner that endeared him to most people. Like Robbie, Rogers collected 'Business Partners' who brought money and cars into his business. Rogers only contribution was his office, his staff (me) and his contacts. Everything they sold would go through his own private company first and then be bought by the new company formed by Rogers and his new partners. This ensured that whatever happened Rogers himself couldn't lose, he would get the commission and profit twice.

Rogers and his partners would have long meetings in his office and I would take notes, it looked good as I had a shorthand notebook but I made up my own version of shorthand as I went along. They had deep discussions about selling strategies and policies and then the partners would leave on expeditions to sell whatever it was at the time all over London, the Home Counties and the North of England. When they were ready to leave Rogers would say, "I'm staying back to give Peter some dictation and then I am leaving for Scotland." Then as soon as they left he would tell me "If you want me I am with Shelley, or whichever girl was lucky that day, but if my wife or the bank rings or any of those other men call, just say I am in Scotland and you don't know when I'll be back."

With that he would go and sometimes not return to the office for a week or more.

I went in to the office every day and sat reading books, waiting for the telephone to ring and calling Vincent who was at home or I went through his files re-reading all those letters. Rogers telephoned every so often to check that no one was after him.

Rogers brought several girls to our flat in Wandsworth Common and often used one of the bedrooms overnight. There was the beautiful Trinidadian who afterwards followed him into exile in Spain when he finally left his wife and debts taking all the cash he could muster. The Brazilian beauty who giggled all night and screamed during her orgasms which seemed to be every half hour.

But the most memorable, a tall, legs up to everywhere, brunette from Yorkshire, a teacher I think, they made such a fantastic looking couple, both of them so tall and looking so self-assured and confident. Jane was in her twenties and Rogers was the first man she had slept with besides her Father with whom she had had a love affair since she was a child.

This had been no forced child abuse, she was just in love with her Father and he with her. Even while she was seeing Rogers she telephoned her Father every day as if she just had to hear his voice. She seemed to be trying Rogers as a sort of reverse therapy but eventually she went back to her family home to be with her Father who was the man she really loved. The Mother was in the house but merely tolerated by the husband and daughter, they were so much in love the mother was just a nuisance to them.

One of our neighbours in Wandsworth Common had some Siamese cats, there were rumours that she bred them to excess and kept them all in cages in one of her rooms.

Always on the look out for ways to make some money I thought it would be nice to have one myself and breed from it. I searched the Exchange & Mart and eventually bought a Seal Point that had some Blue Point in her ancestry. The lady who sold her to me brought her down from Southall herself and then shortly afterwards her daughter appeared. "Just to make sure the cat has settled down," is how she put it but I think her mother had mentioned that I was living with a black man and she was anxious to investigate. Rogers was in the flat when she called and her face lit up and they began a close friendship almost at once. There was a lot of prejudice at the time but also a lot of interest from some people. An old lady living next door to us told Rogers "There wasn't anyone as nice as you when I was young, I think I was born too early." There is no doubt that Rogers could 'charm'.

The first mating with Jasmine the cat was not a success. I had taken her to a man in Shepherds Bush who was a bit eccentric and left her for three days but soon after the mating she had a cold and the vet gave her penicillin which I now believe acted as a birth control so the kittens didn't appear. I had to take her back to the stud cat but this time to make sure I was going to leave her for a week.

When we went in she took one look at the stud cat and disappeared under a table but I just left her and somehow it happened and she came home pregnant.

She had six beautiful kittens that she insisted on bringing to me in my bed.

Only two were Seal Point and the other four Blue Point, for a few weeks it was like living with a herd of mini elephants as they charged around the place but they were soon big enough to sell. On the day I sold the last one Jasmine took sick and died, I never knew why as I didn't take her to the vet, we buried her in the garden with her favourite toys and that was the end of cat breeding for us.

So many things were happening in the 60's, apart from my own different lifestyle so many other things were going on. The radio was swamped by songs from a new group called 'The Beatles' and in Wardour Street Rogers was importing a hot selling line in counterfeit Beetles souvenirs, anything with a beetle on it was a sure seller. Some sad things as well in 1962, first Marilyn Monroe died in the August and then in the November her idol and hero to all of us J.F. Kennedy was killed. This was such a shock to me, I had been so proud of him being the first Catholic President of the United States and Black people there had achieved such a breakthrough during his presidency. It was very cold that winter of 62/3 and unlike our Jamaican friends who had become independent British Guiana was having some problems and in June 1963 we began getting news of riots in Georgetown.

I was still working for Rogers but working at home. For some time the calls from the bank had gotten more insistent as they tried to contact Rogers. He had purchased the largest yet consignment of lager from Denmark and I knew he didn't have the money to pay for it. After many letters and telephone calls the Director of the Danish firm called in person. Rogers was in the office with me and couldn't escape or hide behind my voice on the telephone. The Danish man, tall and handsome with greyish hair was so polite and kind in his manner. Rogers looked harassed and hunted, but only for a short while, he quickly recovered.

"Mr. Rogers," said the Dane, "We have written to you but cannot get a reply from you, we are very worried about our product, you must have sold it by now."

"Yes," Rogers started. "I have been worried as well and have written many letters to you, haven't I Peter?" He said, turning to me and I lying answered, "Yes of course you have sir." "Your lager has cost me a great deal of money," went on Rogers gathering words around himself in protection. "Something was wrong with that consignment of lager, all my customers have complained that they have had to return money as the lager was not good. I have had to return all their money to them and I also had to pay to take back all the lager and dispose of it."

I knew that all the lager had been good, I also knew that I had sold a lot of it myself but I further realised that if Rogers wasn't paying he wouldn't be able to ask me to pay him for the lagers that we still had stored in our cellar.

Faced with this explanation the Dane did not argue, he was only in London for one day and had to see many other customers and did not really have the time to investigate properly Rogers allegations or visit any of Rogers' customers. I heard him speak the words but could hardly believe that it was true when he said "Mr. Rogers I am so sorry for your inconvenience, we will send you another consignment of lager free of charge to make amends for the last one and we will cancel the account for that one." This meant that Rogers had two shiploads of lager and it hadn't cost him anything. When the Danish man went and we were alone, Rogers danced around the office shouting "Peter, Peter, did you see, how did I do it, I can't believe it." "Nor can I you lucky devil, you had better let me have some cases of the new lager when it arrives." He laughed, "Peter you can have anything you want."

Emboldened by the success of this he turned to the importation of felt tipped pens which were all the rage and soon the office was piled high with boxes of felt tipped pens from Japan.

That was when we had the fire.

Rogers had recently arranged quite a large insurance cover on the office, the contents and me. One morning I arrived at the office to find the door sealed by the Fire Brigade, the man in the shop on the ground floor told me, "A mysterious fire apparently broke out during the night and the whole of the top floors are burnt out."

I went back home and telephoned Rogers at his house in Wimbledon.

"Yes I know Peter, the Fire Brigade telephoned me during the night, don't worry about it. Do you mind if I bring a typewriter to your place and we can work from there?" I didn't mind, it would save me the bother of travelling up to town each day. For about three months after that I worked at home, Rogers called in at odd hours giving me very little to do except copy out invoices in various books and in different styles of handwriting. One day he came and told me that his insurance claim had been settled and he had managed to rescue all the pens from the office and sell them; he talked of buying premises in Stockwell and setting up there in a big way. He didn't come at all the next day and on the morning after that his wife telephoned me to say that she hadn't seen him for days. "Do you know where he is Peter?" she asked me. I told her that he had been in the day before but that I didn't know where he was now, "I thought that he was at home with you," I said, "If I see him before he contacts you I'll make sure he calls you straight away."

But that was the last time any of us saw him, he had left England to live in Malaga with his Trinidadian girlfriend.

CHAPTER SEVEN.

It was getting difficult to obtain news from Guiana, letters were delayed and with no news of his family at home Vincent was very unsettled. We couldn't even get any information through the Red Cross, all we had to go on were newspaper reports of race riots. I didn't quite understand this as in British Guiana there are very few families that are completely of one race, the six races that make up the population are so mixed up that it is not easy to say you don't like one of them.

If you look African you could easily have relatives that are Asian, Amerindian, Chinese, Portugese or White. I didn't know then that my own Father was from the Essequibo and had been a mixture of Black and Indian known in Guiana as 'Dougla' and I am blond.

The boats arriving at Southampton were full of Guyanese who had decided to come to England to live. One of them, Enid, arrived on our doorstep, she had been a friend of Vincent in Georgetown and had come to England to marry her English boyfriend whom she had met when he went to Guiana with the British Forces to police the country for the British Government. In the early 60's Enid had been able to travel without a passport by travelling with a professional family as their maid.

It's hard to imagine now how easy it was then for someone to arrive in the country, but of course Guiana was still 'British' and everyone there had the right to come to England without much question.

Enid was able to confirm a lot about what had happened during the riots and as I had thought it was more political than racial. Although British Guiana had been owned by the British Government it had in fact been run by the sugar interests.

When sugar beet production started to take off in Europe they had begun to run down the sugar estates as not being profitable. Without much other sources of income, unemployment would naturally lead to unrest, add to this the political uncertainties of what would happen about independence and there were ready made causes of disturbance. When the problems started of course the people in Georgetown too advantage of the situation. They looted the shops and carried away all the things they couldn't normally afford, as most of the businesses were run by Asians did make the riots appear racial in nature. Having looted the shops most of the houses were full of luxury imported items and bolts of cloth. But when things started to quieten down and the British troops and policemen began to search the houses for looted goods all the trenches and canals were full and clogged up as everyone dumped their spoils in order to save their skins. Enid and her Grandmother quickly cut their bolts of cloth and made rough dresses which they hung on washing lines in the yard to take down and complete when the soldiers had gone. During the fighting Enid had been shot and a bullet was lodged in her shoulder, but she had met her Englishman and as soon as he was transferred back to England she went up to Colchester to marry him. For the short time she stayed with us she proved an asset, helping Vincent behind the bar encouraging the men to buy her shots of whisky that she didn't drink but hid so that they could be sold again.

With Rogers out of the country and no-one else that we knew taking his place importing lager, we went back to buying our supplies from the breweries but we became a bit too successful for our own good. The authorities had become aware of the extent of parties like ours where alcohol was sold and had started to clamp down. The local papers were full of reports of police raids and they not only confiscated the alcohol but also any money that you had taken as well. One Saturday night we had a really great party that exceeded our usual crowds.

Unfortunately some men got very drunk and a fight started, the fight went on and on until it spilled out into the street and up along the road into the next street.

I begged all of them, "Hit each other if you must but don't make so much noise when you do it." Of course I was ignored, the only thing that happened was that they all said keep Peter out of the way and make sure he is O.K. The next morning when I went out to get the Sunday Papers I saw that all the gardens in the street had their share of bottles; luckily none of our neighbours associated it with us but Vincent and I talked about it and decided that we would have to withdraw from the party scene and just sell drinks quietly. "I don't want to face those crowds, work hard to get that money and then have the police raid us and take it away," I told Vincent, "We will have to think of something else."

To help make up the missing income Vincent managed to get a job working at Normansfield, a psychiatric hospital somewhere in Hampton Wick, He didn't stay long though and I could understand why. So many of the other nurses were not very pleasant to the patients and Vincent came home with many tales of patients being hit with brushes and straps, it seemed to be a place of abandonment. Some of the patients there were members of extremely wealthy and well-known families who had sent them there to keep them out of sight. This seemed to me to be the worst thing imaginable, these were families that could have paid for someone to care for them at home but instead chose to send them to state institutions just as if they had nobody to care for them.

In that summer of 65, a friend of Vincent's came back from holiday in Guiana with a parcel for Vincent from a mutual friend in Georgetown, Vincent was very excited at receiving the parcel and said, "This is it at last, now I can really make some money in this Britain." He wouldn't tell me what it was or let me see it and for some reason that I can't explain I thought it best not to insist and then I just forgot about it.

That was how his speculum came.

The Government was encouraging us all to buy houses and it was possible to buy a property without any money for a deposit and without any proof of income. The money came mainly from the G.L.C. but some boroughs like Lewisham were also encouraging people to buy houses like mad. I had always wanted us to buy a house but our income was so unsure, I never knew when or where we would get money even to live on. Then I saw an advertisement for maisonettes in Wivenhoe near Colchester that I was sure we could afford.

I got the details and one Sunday we both went up to Colchester on the train from Liverpool Street, a bus went from there to Wivenhoe passing the new Essex University, down leafy lanes until we reached the site where the maisonettes were in the process of being built. I fell in love with the way they were situated.

Opposite was a farm, I could see rabbits and birds and right next door was an old timbered country pub. Vincent encouraged me to go ahead with the purchase and said how nice we could make the place. The maisonettes only had one bedroom so we assumed that they would be bought by other couples like us or by single people, but when we did move in it was chaos. All the other maisonettes had been sold to couples with children, their single bedrooms had been divided up into two and the sitting rooms had beds in them. After moving in we only stayed for two weeks, it was awful with that many people, added to that the isolation after living in the heart of London was hard to take; to do any shopping we had to take a bus into Colchester, the fares were expensive, we weren't working, had no money and unlike London no means of making any.

One morning we just packed up and went back to Balham and tried to find somewhere to live but it wasn't easy. After a fruitless search I went to stay with Ken and Brenda in Crouch Hill and Vincent went to stay with one of his cousins in Stoke Newington. Neither of us was comfortable, I was slightly the better off, Brenda made me very welcome but I had to sleep on a folding bed in the sitting room, in those days most of us lived in private rented accommodation, which was never large. Vincent had to sleep with one of his cousin's grandchildren in a house full of noisy young children and he wasn't used to that. We stuck it out for about three weeks and then we found a room in Muswell Hill but it wasn't nice at all. The landlord and the room was pleasant enough but the smell of the house was off putting. All the other tenants were single men working in the building trade, the bathroom facilities could not cope with so many men even though most of them didn't seem to bathe much anyway. At night the window ledges were decorated with their boots that they placed there to cool off from the days exertions. Vincent made regular trips to Balham in search of a room and eventually managed to rent a room in a house in Huron Road where he had stayed before. We packed and moved without even waiting to get back the deposit that we had had to pay for the front door keys and gradually settled into another phase of our life.

The maisonette in Wivenhoe was left empty and we only went there occasionally to make sure that it was secure. The only person to use the place was Willy and his girlfriend Eve. Willy was working at a dry cleaners in Battersea where Eve was the manageress. The owner of the dry cleaners had several shops all run by manageresses who were also his lovers. Each one of them thinking that this was the only shop and they were the only lover, except for Eve who found out at the same time that Willy went to work in her shop, they fell in love and went up to Wivenhoe leaving the shop owner and Angela, Willy's wife. Willy was fated by his attraction to and from women.

He left his wife to live permanently with Eve and eventually after countless public rows, Angela divorced him and he married Eve. They moved to a quiet Sussex village to what Eve imagined would be an idyllic life but having made love with the wife of the most respected man in the village, both Willy and the wife were suffocated by the fumes from the car in his own garage.

They had foolishly left the motor running to warm the garage so that they could make love naked. Soon after I first met Willy I asked him why he went with so many women, "I can't help myself, I just need the stimulation," he told me, "And look Peter how small I am." He pulled down his zip and showed me his cock, it was fairly small. "The women are worse than me," he went on, "When they see this little thing they can't resist it, they are sure it can't do them any harm."

Vincent too was having relationships, but with boys. He also needed the stimulation I suppose. He came home late one night and told me that he had spent hours in a police station in the West End. "What on earth for Vincent, what did you do?" "I was just in Victoria Station minding my own business when this policeman came up, grabbed me, and said that I was importuning." I didn't understand this and asked him what he had been doing there anyway. He confessed that he had met an Italian boy and they had arranged to meet at Victoria. The boy hadn't been there and Vincent had just waited around hoping that he would eventually turn up.

The police assumed that he was just there waiting to be picked up, maybe he was but he insisted to me that he had just been waiting for his friend.

Vincent had given the police a false name and they gave him bail on his own recognizance to turn up in court. He didn't go and for the next four weeks only went out at night and then with a hat pulled well down over his face.

It should have upset me I suppose but Vincent skulking around like a criminal in a B movie appealed to my sense of the ridiculous, soon we forgot about it and the incident passed into memory.

While I was staying in Crouch Hill with Ken and Brenda I managed to get a job with one of the largest credit reference and debt collecting agencies in the country, The London and Provincial Trade Protection Society. This was before the age of the computer and all the records were maintained manually, I spent a lot of time searching through the files for the names of people I knew. This was very interesting especially when I saw all the variations of Rogers' name that they had and as everything was filed in strict alphabetical order none of them had been Cross-referenced, only I knew they were all connected. My real work there wasn't very interesting as it consisted mainly of adding up columns of figures which I could never balance anyway. The office, in Berners Street, was very old fashioned, run by a strict lady who wouldn't let us use adding machines – believing that adding up by hand was more accurate. Hardly anyone else liked her but when I told her that I was living with a black friend she reciprocated the confidence by telling me about her black niece and let my many adding mistakes pass without too much comment. Then after six months they transferred me to the Croydon office, very modern with dozens of young girls manning the accounting machines. Most of these girls were on diets (they said), these diets consisted of diet chocolate and biscuit meals which they ate immediately after coming back from lunch usually comprising something fried and accompanied by chips and buttered rolls. They were convinced that by eating the diet chocolate they would be slim enough to eat anything they wished. The thought that the chocolate was to be used as a substitution for a meal didn't occur to them. I stayed there as long as I could but the combination of the empty headed girls and the awkward journey didn't suit me and I left without another job to go to.

It wasn't too bad as Vincent and I were now making wedding cakes and had some money coming in. He showed me how to ice cakes and make the sugar roses that he used lavishly to decorate the cakes. Some of the brides liked to come to us before the wedding to get into their dresses or have their hair styled. We did everything for them, calming nerves and applying face packs. I also started making hats, well at least I trimmed them. While I had been working in Wardour Street I had noticed a shop selling hat shapes which I found easy to cover with material. Most of the material I used came from a Barbadian dressmaker who had his workshop over a shop opposite Clapham Junction station.

Darriel was Vincent's friend, he was more than a dressmaker, he was a genius with cloth. His customers came to him clutching cuttings from magazines or papers showing the style of dress they wanted. Darriel, after taking just a quick look at the picture, would measure the client, lay out the material on his bench and just cut out the pieces and sew them immediately. No fittings were every necessary, no matter how complex the design or how many pieces made up some of the more intricate designs the garment would fit exactly to perfection.

On Friday and Saturday nights Darriel sold drinks and souse which is a favourite dish in Barbados made from pigs head, heavily peppered and garnished with raw onions and cucumbers. Darriel himself got roaring drunk, all the time sitting at his sewing machine making the most fabulous clothes.

Vincent was careful not to let me go there too often as Darriel made no effort to his liking for me and when he was drinking would often announce, "If anything happens to Vincent I am going to marry Peter and look after him."

Although Darriel had a wife and children he was considered most eligible by both the men and women that went to his house.

As I still had the mortgage to pay on the maisonette (Vincent was never good with bills) I went to the Labour Exchange to see if they could find me another job. At first I had no luck but one afternoon I had a special interview with the manager who suggested the Tax Office. I didn't think they would employ me, I had had so many jobs since leaving school – but fortunately I had gone to the Labour Exchange in Colchester and my file had been transferred there. The local office in Tooting had made no record of the transfer so I had a brand new file just showing the one job with L.A.P.P.T. I started work with the Inspector of Taxes as a clerical assistant. This was a nice job and only ten minutes away from home. This was another old-fashioned office awash with papers to be filed, checked and accounted for. As a clerical assistant I was at the bottom of the ladder, all I had to do was filing and answer the public counter when the bell rang. I quickly settled down, the best friend I had there was a lady from Battersea, Hilda, she was slim, perky, about five feet tall with red rinsed hair and wore those tarty shoes with stiletto heels and always wore a fur stole when she went to the pub. Hilda was a clerical assistant as well but from her manner and the way she bossed the other assistants, visitors to the office were under the impression that she was the Inspector. There was always a lot of movement among the higher ranks and when the female Inspector left and was replaced by a racy Scotsman, Hilda struck gold. They immediately became friends and he relied on her to keep him abreast of the gossip around the office and who was doing what and with whom. I got on with him as well, he was a very kind and considerate boss but the rest of the staff were not so sure. They were very insular and a Scotsman was nearly as bad as a black man to them. Yes they were extremely prejudiced, but for some reason weren't prejudiced against me even though I was living openly with a black man.

The more the rest of the staff showed their unease with the Inspector, the more Hilda and I became closer to him, this had many benefits, as Hilda was very aware.

Hilda and I would go to lunch early at 11am and often get back to the office after 3pm. "Peter and I have been to lunch with the Inspector," Hilda would announce to the office in reply to the raised eyebrows and none too subtle glances at the clock by the clerical officers who were our seniors but who were not too sufficiently confident of their own position with the Inspector to raise any question of discipline towards us. Hilda and I ran the tea club and whenever an office party was to be arranged we would naturally be in charge of the catering arrangements. Hilda was an old hand at this, after obtaining the money from the social club or after running weeks of raffles carefully orchestrated by Hilda where I won lots of prizes; we would take hours off from work to shop and prepare. We bought the largest sizes of everything that could be remotely connected with the food we were going to prepare. Back in the office in our little filing room we would divide up the spoils and leave that night with laden bags, Hilda announcing, "Peter is going to help by doing a lot of cooking at home as we have no facilities here and we want the party to be a success."

The fact that the food we did have at these parties owed more to J.Lyons than to Hilda and me went unremarked by the rest of the staff who were somewhat in awe of Hilda who like Vincent had her own version of facts. At the parties we usually had a bar and to make it seem legal and avoid breaking any licensing laws it was suggested that we issue tickets and during the party exchange tickets for drinks, so avoiding the necessity of charging and collecting money during the evening. This always started out according to plan, but after a few rounds of drinks and when they ran out of tickets Hilda and I just sold the drinks and theoretically when we balanced our books the next day we should have had enough money to pay the off licence for the drinks that we always took on sale or return. We never did have enough money.

"We think someone was taking drinks without paying for them, " or "someone must have taken those three bottles of spirits we had in reserve," we would blandly assert as we went around the office collecting money for the shortfall. There was usually enough money left after settling the off licence bill for Hilda and I to visit the pub in Chestnut Grove and have lunch and quite a few drinks.

"Well I think we deserve it Peter, after all we take on the responsibility of these things, no-one else wants to do it." Hilda would say this in all seriousness knowing full well that not one of our fellow workers would dare suggest any changes in the way Hilda ran the office.

Vincent liked me working so near to home, he was very possessive and took great pains to try to know exactly where I was and with whom. If I went to the pub at lunchtime, with people from the Tax Office, by the time I got home he would know how long I had been in there and just who I had been there with. The 'Freemasonry' of the Caribbean community worked very well for him, it was impossible for me to even get on a bus and not have someone see me and tell him. If we were at a party and someone not from the family or close circle of friends came to talk to me, Vincent would be told, "That man is talking very close to Peter, see who it is."

Vincent would suddenly appear next to me so that the stranger would be under no misapprehension but that I was out of bounds. Everybody co-operated with Vincent. I didn't know then, but later I found out, that Vincent had a hold on most of the people that he knew; so many of them confided in him in one way or another and he knew all their secrets.

The house in Huron Road was in multiple occupation as most of them were in those days. Six families with one bathroom caused a problem with cleaning, the only good thing about the house was that we all had our own cooking facilities in our rooms. At first we lived in a room on the ground floor but then two rooms became vacant on the middle floor of the house which was more convenient for us as we were making cakes for large weddings at the time. One particular wedding nearly turned out to be a disaster. The man from the Gas Board came in the morning to read the meter, which was prepaid so there was always a rebate due.

He left a pile of silver in the bathroom and the three of us there at the time agreed to give the rebate to one tenants who had had the meter in his room broken into and who had to repay all the money that had been taken. We were all under pressure with money then but Ritchie was a favourite neighbour, very kind, thoughtful and like most of us in the house living in a mixed relationship, but we all agreed his white girlfriend was a hopeless case and that he had taken on a lot of responsibility with her as she had come to him with two children of her own which Ritchie cared for as if they were his.

We thought that we had done the right thing but there was another tenant, Dorothy, living in a back room on the ground floor with her husband and child who never did fit in with the rest of us. She hadn't been there when we decided what to do with the gas money and when she came home in the evening she took umbrage that she had not been consulted. Vincent, who had not been there either, took the full weight of her outrage. There must have been a previous misunderstanding that we didn't know about that made her react in the way that she did. Dorothy flew at Vincent calling him a fucking thief. He retaliated in no uncertain terms saying that she was "A whore who was never dry from all the men that went with her, your husband is a fool if he cannot see what you are up to. Just because you can go with plenty of white men that you meet in the street doesn't mean that you are any good."

The air was blue, the language descriptive with much posturing on both sides, she, Dorothy, in the downstairs hall marching up and down in her rage and he, Vincent, moving up and down the staircase in concert with her. In vain I and the other tenants tried to explain what had happened but neither of them were in the mood to listen and after some hours both contestants retired to their respective quarters and the matter might have died a natural death as these things do if Vincent hadn't made the reference during the quarrel to the fact that Dorothy was in the habit of meeting white men at work and in the street and while not exactly prostituting, she did do the next best thing in an amateurish way. Of course she had to protect herself from future gossip which might have jeopardized her relationship with her husband who was already jealous and suspicious regarding some items of new clothing that had appeared without comment from Dorothy. The man was tall and heavy like a bull and whatever version Dorothy told him was effective. He charged up the stairs, pushing straight through our glass kitchen door and into the bed sitting room to tackle Vincent who by this time had grabbed a heavy soda bottle stand and pounded Elcocks head with a vengeance. Elcock retired bleeding and Dorothy took over from him but Vincent hit her on the head with a glass jug raising a bump as big as a grapefruit. By this time the place was in a shambles, furniture and glass everywhere, the cakes in the kitchen were covered in glass fragments and Vincent was covered in blood. I was scared and left the house to run to the corner telephone to call the police, on my way I was accompanied by neighbours already with their own versions of the fight even if they hadn't witnessed it themselves.

"That man nearly killed Vincent, he is covered with blood! Oh my God, poor Vincent."

"That's right Peter, you call the police, you can't do anything yourself. We'll go back with you and tell the police what happened."

"It's a good thing that Elcock didn't go for you as well, you couldn't handle him as well as Vincent."

I got through to 999 and gave the police my version of what had happened and then ran back to the house fearing that worse might be happening but by the time I got back the police were already there. In the short time that it took for them to arrive Elcock had washed his face and had changed into a clean shirt and trousers and looked comparatively unharmed but Vincent was still standing in the middle of the sitting room, still angry, shouting a lot and covered with Elcocks blood. Vincent really looked the part of the victim whereas Elcock looked like a cool bully. The policeman offered to take Vincent to the hospital but he declined and after cleaning his face it was clear that he had suffered nothing more than bruised dignity and he continued his outraged version of the fight to an ever-increasing crowd of neighbours and friends who came to hear the account. Poor Elcock, really the victim of his wife's foolishness, had to make his own way to the hospital where he had to have fifteen stitches in his head.

The landlord wasn't keen on replacing all the broken glass and thought that we should do it, but as we had neither the money or the inclination thinking that if anyone should pay it should be the Elcocks. We assumed, rightly or wrongly that we were the aggrieved party and I was outraged at the suggestion of us paying as I had been very frightened during the whole affair even though I had kept well out of the actual fray and had suffered no physical damage. The knowledge that someone had been strong enough to break through the door filled me with a dread.

After a thorough examination of the cakes we decided that we could probably use them after all and armed with my eyebrow tweezers I removed all the pieces of glass that I could see and we iced the cakes for the bride. We told everyone that we had to bake fresh cakes as Elcock had destroyed the others, when I went shopping in Balham Market it took me much longer now as I had to give all and sundry my version of what had happened.

We heard in a roundabout way that Elcock had been advised to summons Vincent because of his head injuries but that he was unwilling to do so. Vincent said, "Just in case he does do something like that I think we should summons him and get our side in first." We found a firm of solicitors at Amen Corner in Tooting where we were dealt with by a blunt Englishman who first tended to deal more with me than with Vincent – probably because I was white. After establishing that Vincent was the one directly involved with the actual fighting he decided that the best course of action was to use Vincent's name in the summons against the Elcocks and to use me as a witness.

The solicitor advised us very well, "You Peter, tell me what happened that day."

I related the background to the start of the argument between Vincent and Dorothy and when I said that Dorothy swore he said, "I suppose she did, what words did she use?" "Well you know," I hesitated to use the words. "No I don't know, " he said lowering his eyebrows at me, "and when you get to court the Magistrate won't know either unless you repeat exactly what she said."

"She said that we were fucking thieves."

"That's better, now you mustn't be afraid to say that in court."

He made me repeat all the fucks and obscenities that Dorothy had used that day and said that when asked I should repeat them loudly and clearly. As he said these were not my words but the words of the woman who attacked Vincent. When the Elcocks received the summons they counter summoned and our solicitor called us into his office to ask if there had been any other witnesses. I told him that as far as I knew the only other tenants at home that night had been Brenda and Ritchie. He wanted to know if either of them was white and when I said Brenda he asked me for a description of her. When he heard that Brenda was from Sheffield he wanted to know what she sounded like. "She has a nice northern accent," I said. "Don't worry about her then, you will have to be the only witness, the court will not listen to someone they cannot understand easily." Both Vincent and I appreciated the Solicitor's blunt behaviour, we were still many years from local accents on the radio and these were the days when open prejudice was accepted and black people and regional accents were not thought to be reliable.

On the day of the case Balham Magistrates court was packed with our friends and neighbours and a few of Elcocks friends. Even when you attend a court as an innocent party it is still overwhelming and I was a bit nervous. For some reason of procedure the Elcocks appeared before we did but they were both overawed by the occasion and toned down their language to suit. When it was my turn to enter the witness box I played to the gallery and gave my evidence in loud clear tones, repeating all the swear words and curses clearly, the way the solicitor had told me to do. I noticed the Magistrate looking approvingly at my courage in repeating the words. Dorothy paled when I spoke, she had not expected that I would repeat those words in public. Everything went well for us, the Magistrate was an experienced man who we were to meet later on a more serious occasion. We were awarded the cost of repairs and the cost of the cakes, we also learned that in an English court it is wise to have an English barrister to speak on your behalf. The Elcocks used a Black barrister with an accent that wasn't easy to understand and consequently wasn't listened to. By the same token, if I was to need a barrister in the Caribbean or in Africa I would certainly not let an English lawyer near me. I know that things are supposed to have changed but I am not so sure of that. Although we had won the case and the Elcocks paid their fine without any problems, the atmosphere in the house had changed and neither Vincent nor I felt comfortable living there.

To ensure that Dorothy didn't recommence hostilities I burnt a lot of incense sticks, pushing them into the doorframe so that the smell drifted downstairs to her room.

This was effective, Dorothy was convinced, she told a friend, "Those boys are using 'Obeah' against me." She was aware that Guyanese are large practitioners of The African 'Obeah' religion. (1)

Aunt Carrie's granddaughter, Lotys was about to leave for Canada with her husband and son Gregory. They had been living in the top half of a house in Streatham, the owner of the house was a Guyanese man, James and his wife Lynette, who we had met several times and we arranged to take over the flat when Lotys left.

This was a large Edwardian house overlooking Tooting Bec Common and we were very happy to leave the strained atmosphere of Huron Road.

On the day we moved out and while some of our things were in the hall, Dorothy made one last stand and taking a hammer broke the glass in a china cabinet. If she hoped to provoke an incident she lost out, we just ignored her but before I left I sprinkled salt over the doorstep to give her something to think about when we had gone.

(1)*'Obeah' is the Caribbean and particularly Guyanese practice of what is known in Europe as witchcraft. Practioners of the art use ancient methods brought with the slaves from Africa who use potions and incantations to cure illness or provide protection; but most often to ensure the affections or faithfulness of someone you love. Burning incense cleans the house and salt sprinkled on your doorstep kills the power of any Obeah magic brought in by an enemy. Banned by the British, Obeah was given religious status by the Burnham Government.'*

CHAPTER EIGHT.

As always when we made a move I had the feeling that this time we would be lucky and thing would work out better for us. The main problem was Vincent's jealousy, in order that I would not have any thoughts about a friendship with James, the landlord, who was a most attractive sexy looking man, he told me that James didn't really like me but only accepted me as a friend of Vincent's and that if I upset him he, James, would ask us to leave. For a long time I was ill at ease in James presence and not until later when Vincent was in prison did I find out that James liked both of us equally.

Vincent's jealousy was a one-way thing that led to much fighting and arguments, we were so hot blooded when we were young and seemed to be fighting most of the time. Although Vincent felt so strongly about me it didn't stop him from looking for and finding young men to entertain. While we were in the flat at Wandsworth Common he had met a young Dutchman, Robert, who was infatuated with Vincent so much that he called at the flat everyday and telephoned constantly, crying and telling Vincent how much he loved him. Somehow I didn't object, we still had as much sex as ever and I was so confident of his love for me. One night I remember we had a terrible fight over nothing at all really, but once we started we broke everything in the flat, glass, china and windows.

We tore each other's clothing and pulled out each others hair screaming the most terrible things at each other. Although I didn't think that I was jealous most probably deep down I was. In the middle of this big fight the doorbell rang and there was Robert, the Dutchman. Robert took in the scene and his face lit up, it was as if Christmas and all his birthdays had come at once, it was a joy to see, he left quickly – probably to hug the thought of this break-up to his heart and wait for the next day when he would come and claim his love. Unfortunately for him, his coming broke the mood and before he had time to reach the end of the street we were in bed making love with a passion that left us exhausted and in a rosy glow the next morning. Even when we fought it was like making love, we could play each other like a fisherman plays with a trout. It was like being in a maze and we knew all the exits; whatever happened we were destined to remain together.

Robert confided to a mutual friend, "Poor Vincent, that Peter treats him so badly.

Vincent would like to leave him but Peter won't let him go not even after they had that terrible fight." The friend more knowledgeable told him, "Don't you understand that Peter and Vincent are never going to leave each other no matter what happens."

We were like that throughout all the years we were together, always coupled in everyone's mind. I should have been more jealous but I felt as if each of his conquests were somehow mine as well and I encouraged him in everything he did as if he were an extension of myself. I was so confident that he would always be around, our families knew each other and I made no pretence about our relationship either where I worked or where we lived.

I hoped that in Streatham we could expand the cake making business as I felt that with Vincent's attitude towards daily employment our best way forward would be to work for ourselves, although he did seem to have money and when I asked him how he explained it by saying that "Bill has plenty of money and he is very generous to me." Bill was a journalist that Vincent had become friendly with, apparently just out of the kindness of his heart he gave Vincent large sums of money for nothing.

I knew there was something else but as Vincent was strong enough to cope and didn't pay any less attention to me I just let it pass.

We had tried a business before while we were in Wandsworth Common. After we opted out of the party giving I started looking for something that we could do together and found a snack bar for sale in Brockley. The vendor was nice and he was only asking a hundred or so pounds, he agreed to accept monthly payments without any deposit. I soon realised that he was only too pleased to be out of his agreement with British Rail who owned the property. It really was a bad move but at the time it was exciting for us. Willy, the Grenadian, helped us to clean up the place and move our things in. It was really nothing more than a hut but as it was on the main road and near to the station we thought it would be all right.

Vincent said, "We are on the way to making our fortune" and I believed him.

For the next few months we spent every Sunday baking in preparation for the week ahead, but success was not to be, at least not there. We had few customers as a newer establishment had opened even nearer the station and was more equipped than we were. Looking back we were lucky that the environment people hadn't taken an interest in us. There were no toilet facilities and no main drainage, the washing up water had to be collected in a bucket and sluiced into the kerb to drain away. We were burgled and our stock of cigarettes taken, then one morning we arrived there to find that rats had eaten into our stocks of food and chocolate bars.

This was depressing to say the least and we decided to call it a day and leave.

Somehow we had only made two payments to the vendor and no rent at all to British Rail. I advertised it as a good going concern at double what we paid.

It was amazingly easy to sell, several people wanted to buy and I sold it to a man who was putting his daughter into business; he paid cash – two hundred and fifty pounds. This was a week before Christmas, we paid the rent and set about to celebrate Christmas in style. Amongst the friends we asked to help us celebrate was Helene. Helene came from Indonesia via Holland, she had entangled herself with a wretch of a man from British Guiana who have her a baby and then left her. To support herself and the baby girl she moved to Chelmsford and travelled every day to Oxford Street to work in a store and then every evening she stayed on to work in theatres and again on Saturdays and Sundays. She had not been getting more than two hours sleep each night and Vincent suggested that she spent some nights with us to save on travelling. We decided to invite her with her baby for the whole Christmas period. With Vincent's sister and her friend and six others we had a houseful for Christmas day. We spent all the money. I bought a small record player, we had duck, goose, chicken, pork, turkey, beef and pepperpot. Pepperpot is the most famous Guyanese dish and comprises of various meats and spices cooked with casareep which is a seasoning made from cassava root. Vincent made an enormous cake, mince patties and sausage rolls. I bought nuts, sweets, biscuits – everything I could think of. In all our years together I think it was the best Christmas we have ever had, so much food and drink and all our bills paid, it was heaven that December. The most amazing thing of all was that we heard no more about the snack bar, nothing from British Rail, nothing from the vendor and nothing from the man who bought it from us. What a relief it was not to have it hanging over our heads.

We settled down in the Streatham house and started to get it nicely furnished, Vincent went to a large furniture shop in Clapham and bought a three piece suite, a large oval dining table and several occasional tables. He only made a small down payment and shortly afterwards the shop closed, I don't know what kind of accounting system they had but he only made that one payment and wasn't asked for any more money. I bought a large second hand commercial size gas stove very cheaply down at Amen

Corner that I think cost about £6, I hoped it would be well used with our cake making.

Vincent announced to me that he was going to help women with their problems.

"What problems Vincent?" I asked him.

"Personal things," he answered "like when they have trouble with a boyfriend or husband." When I asked him how, he said "You've heard about Obeah haven't you, I have lots of friends who have been Obeah men and I know what to do."

He slipped into a lifestyle that suited him, staying in bed until about 4 o'clock, if anyone was coming to see him they would come at that time, then around 7pm he disappeared into the bathroom re-appearing an hour and a half later ready to go out.

Sometimes I would ask, "Where are you going tonight, can't I come with you?"

"I am only going to see Mrs. Lewis about her box money," he would say or "Bill has been given an extra ticket for a show," knowing that I was not keen on going to the theatre he was on safe ground. Mostly I didn't even bother to ask, since moving we had acquired a television and I watched that a lot. I knew anyway that he could always make up some reason for his absence – like the time he left home at 7pm to borrow a pint of rice from Cousin Iris in Balham, returning home at 9am in the morning with the excuse that "It rained and I had to shelter."

When I told Iris she laughingly said, "Well he did come here but left immediately saying he was on his way out." For years afterwards, whenever we met she asked me "Peter, tell me about the rice."

It was mostly women who came to see Vincent for this 'Obeah' work but sometimes couples came or even a man on his own. In the kitchen sometimes there would be bottles of water or some other clear liquid containing eggs floating inside and Vincent gathered a collection of pills and powders that he folded into paper parcels that the women would take with them when they left, clutching them like a talisman. This he told me was all part of the 'Obeah'.

That first Christmas in Streatham he decided to take a holiday in Italy and Germany.

Vincent didn't ask if I would like to go, he just said he was going. He used the 'Box Money' he was holding for a friend, for his fare.

'A Box' is the name used in Guyana for a sort of loan club or unofficial Credit Union. A Box holder collected the money each week from a group of people and each week or month it is someone's turn to receive the total money handed in for that week or month. These Boxes sometimes amount to large sums and continue for a year or more. It is crucial that the holder is extremely trustworthy and is someone who can control his members. One of Vincent's cousins ran one but she had many problems with it and was not a popular box holder as often if you joined it you were the only one. Vincent was very popular with his Box but this particular December he told his friend that I had the money, but he didn't tell me and I had to disappoint the friend when he asked me for it. I thought that he would be angry, he was but not for long, none of Vincent's friends stayed upset with him for long.

Vincent had met an Indian man staying at a large

bed and breakfast house in Balham. He had a German friend staying there and they recommended Vincent to stay with their friend in Hamburg when he went there. As Vincent was going abroad I went to Yorkshire to spend a few days with my Mother and had a lazy time eating chocolates and watching television. When I got home the flat was full of people, Vincent had told the German, Ralf, that he could use the flat whenever he liked; it was news to me and I let them know that I was upset. After Ralf and his friends left I drank rather a lot and was a little woozy when the Indian man came back to apologise. He was so sweet and I was in need of comfort. He soon insisted that it was time that I went to bed and further insisted that he accompany me! At first I was worried and thought that I shouldn't let him see me but then I remembered all of Vincent's friends through the last year also remembering that hackneyed phrase 'What's sauce for the goose is sauce for the gander' and relaxed and enjoyed the attention. Somehow we kept our little romance secret, even though I often met him in the company of Ralf and other friends none of them guessed that later in the night Kapoor came to my bed and changed from his daytime role of dull married professor to enchanting lover with staying power and a technique that lifted me to a high peak of pleasure. When Vincent returned home he had stories of sexual encounters on the Spanish Steps in Rome and in Florence, this time I could hear his tales with pleasure now that I had something to remember as well. Although Vincent had many sexual adventures whilst abroad, he carefully checked the post and kept an ear on the telephone so that he would know if I had been seeing anyone while he had been away, subtly questioning his family and friends to find out what I had been doing. By this time Kapoor had left for Canada and a new teaching post, thankfully nobody was aware of our friendship.

Ralf had come to London in order to escape the German military conscription, his Father had managed to arrange for him to join Merryl Lynch the big stockbrokers to learn the business. His family had a large department store in Hamburg, they met Vincent and liked him very much, inviting him to their home for several meals which according to Vincent were served in different rooms each time, all sumptuously furnished which suited Vincent's snobbish nature.

The boarding house in Balham was run by an elderly lady bent double with arthritis, she did her best but Ralf wasn't accustomed to the baked bean school of catering that she provided. Lynette, James Wife, suggested that Ralf should take the vacant room at the top of the house, and then he could eat with us. This arrangement suited me as well, he agreed to pay me for his food monthly, I left the amount up to him and he gave me enough money to pay for all my shopping. Although he was training he was paid about four times as much as I was. Ralf got on with everyone in the house, he liked the way I cooked and whenever I roasted pork he would appear at my side just as I was about to remove the crackling which he devoured. Vincent had recently acquired another friend, Jan, another Dutchman. Jan was nursing at Springfield hospital and fell in love with Vincent. There was one problem, they were both intent on taking the upper hand so had to settle for being good friends without the romance. Jan gave Vincent an upright piano, neither

Vincent or I could play but Ralf could and insisted on playing 'Deutchland Uber Alles' all the time. Prompted by a mutual dislike with Jan he would play with extra vigour whenever Jan appeared. Ralf had been brought up in the traditional way and knowing that I was in love with Vincent he resented, on my behalf, the way Jan tried to influence Vincent and isolate me. Eventually Jan moved to a North London hospital where he began an affair with an older woman who was able to help his career and in a very short time he moved from nurse to Hospital Superintendent. It was good to have Ralf living in the house, when Vincent went out I had someone to talk to and watch television with, that is unless a sports programme clashed with one of my favourites like 'Adam Adamant' then Ralf would retire sulking to his bedroom. His sulks didn't last long though and he would soon be back downstairs calling "Peter what can I eat please?"

The way to a man's heart!

I came home from work one afternoon at about 4.20, Vincent was in the kitchen with a young white man, probably in his early twenties. Something about him struck a sour note with me and after a brief introduction I went into the sitting room and put on the television. Later, after Vincent had fed him in the kitchen Barry left and Vincent came to sit with me. "Who is that?" I asked, thinking already 'another boyfriend I suppose'. "That is Barry, he has heard that I practice Obeah and he has lots of friends that would be interested, he is coming to talk to me and find out what I can do." I accepted this, what else could I do? To say that I disbelieved him would have led to a lengthy argument and I only wanted a quiet life. Barry became a regular visitor to the house, sometimes with a girlfriend and sometimes the girlfriend would bring two or three other girls who would wait in the sitting room while she consulted Vincent and they would consult him in turn. I didn't like Barry at all, Vincent's explanation was that Barry was interested in Obeah and that he was teaching him. To me it seemed that Barry was more interested in smoking 'funny cigarettes' and popping pills than Obeah and I concluded that they were lovers after all. The thought that Barry and the girls he brought to the house were in the habit of using drugs made me most uncomfortable, I know that at the time I was being prescribed Valium but it didn't seem the same as using illegal drugs on which there was no control. Then Vincent started to talk about buying a car and when I asked him how we would be able to afford one he said that Barry can get cars, that's what he does for a living. I took this to mean that he would steal one and that made me nervous, whenever I saw Barry I had a feeling that something wasn't right.

The tension was making me very out of sorts and I had constant attacks of breathlessness. I took a week off work and spent the time giving the flat a thorough spring clean, the effort made me feel a little more relaxed and on the Monday morning in an effort to be alone with Vincent so that we could talk I suggested that we take a trip to somewhere like Hampton Court. This was a rare morning when Vincent was awake and out of bed before mid-day and although we did go to Hampton Court and have a really good day we didn't talk as I had thought we would. Vincent poo poo'd all my ideas about what was going on although he did agree that the car from Barry would probably be stolen and agreed not to take one from him. Apart from that the most serious thing he would talk about was the assassination of Martin Luther King which had happened on April 4th the same day as my brother's birthday. He said,

"From 1960 up to now in 1968, I wonder if we have really come so far." Vincent was interested in world politics, he had a broader outlook on life than I did; all my main concerns were always closer to home. The weather had become quite warm and I decided to go back to work the next day as I felt relaxed. I had just gone back to the office from having lunch with a new colleague from Pakistan that I had taken under my wing with encouragement from Hilda. The counter bell rang but before I could get to the counter one of the Tax Officers who had been attending to someone came to me and said, "Peter there is a policeman asking for you, what shall I tell him?" My first thought was that something terrible had happened and said not to worry I would go straight away to find out what was the matter. I ran to the counter and the policeman asked "Mr. Simpson?" Yes, yes I answered, tell me what is wrong? Has something happened to my Mother?" He looked at me as if I was a bit thick and said, "no it is not." "But what then?" "I cannot tell you, it is something at home and you must come immediately." I was completely bewildered and out of my depth, I didn't know what it might be. On the way out of the office I told the Inspector that I had to go home straight away as the police had come for me but that I had no idea what was wrong. There were two plain-clothes men in the car with me and we raced through the traffic to Streatham but they wouldn't answer my questions except to say, "We are not allowed to say anything, you must wait until we reach the house." The car screeched to a halt outside the house. Police cars were all around the house and on the grass opposite, they hurried me out of the car and in through the open door. Inside the house men were searching all the rooms, rushing up and down the stairs, all the time shouting to each other. I was led into our bedroom which was in chaos, the cupboards and drawers were all open with clothes and other belongings strewn everywhere. Vincent was sitting on the bed and a small freckle faced man with his face pressed close to Vincent's was shouting questions at him. The noise and confusion was overwhelming. "My giddy aunt," I said, "Vincent what's happened, why are all these men here?" He looked up at me as if he wasn't pleased that I was there and shouted "They are trying to say that someone is dying because of me and this bastard here is standing on my bare foot." He pushed at the short man and shouted with rage at him, "You fucking bastard, you won't let me put my shoes on so that you can hurt me you fucking bully!" He managed to push the man away, jumped up and stood shouting, his face contorted with his anger.

I still didn't know what was going on. "Vincent please calm down and tell me what these people are doing here." "How can I calm down when that pig keeps stamping on my bare feet." I asked the short man, "What is going on and why can't Vincent put on his shoes?"

"Your friend here has performed an illegal operation on a girl, she is losing blood and will probably die."

"An operation, what kind of operation are you talking about?" I was even more bewildered than before, what on earth could he mean. "Don't play games with me," he said, "Your friend performed an abortion and you know it," he went on, "We need to have the instruments he used." I told him, "All the sharp knives are in the kitchen, why not look there and if there has been an operation here where is all the blood?"

He ignored this and asked, "Where is the key to your wardrobe? We need to look inside it." As there wasn't a wardrobe just for me I asked, "Which one do you mean?" He pointed to the small wardrobe that was still closed. "That is just where I hang our shirts," I said, "and it's not locked anyway."

Vincent called out, "You can't look in there that is his personal property."

The officer pulled open the door; one of the men took out all my nicely ironed shirts and threw them down on the floor, I made an effort to rescue them but was stopped by another of the men. After rummaging about in the confusion that was always a feature of our cupboards the officer unearthed an old carrier bag and pulled out from it a shiny tubular thing which I later learnt was a speculum. My God, I thought, that must be the thing his friend brought him back from Guyana some years ago. At least it looked like the same carrier bag. My stomach chilled and I longed for this to finish, thinking that the policemen would soon be gone and then I would work this thing out in my mind. "What is this then, in your wardrobe?" I was asked. "I have no idea what it is and it's not my wardrobe, it just belongs to us." "Your friend here said it was yours. How do you explain that?" I had no reply, I couldn't explain it.

I didn't know that they had been in the house since early morning. One of Barry's girlfriends had been to Vincent and had an abortion. Over the weekend she had bled a lot and gone to a hospital. As was standard practice she had been told that she was dying and they couldn't help her unless they knew who had been involved. As soon as she had given Barry's name they packed her to stop the bleeding and started to treat her. It must have been during our day out at Hampton Court that they tracked down Barry and he in turn had led them to Vincent. When they got to the house on that Tuesday morning Vincent was in the front garden and they just pushed their way in. Vincent denied all knowledge about the abortion but when they asked him if they could look in his room he took them to the top of the house; but after they had been searching for a short while they realised that it was Ralf's room. After searching the whole house, they found most of the things that they later took away, in our bedroom. When they wanted to look in the small wardrobe Vincent had barred it with his body and said, "That is Simpson's wardrobe, it is locked and he has the key." That is how they knew about me living in the house and how they came to the office for me. I was beginning to feel sick; one of the officers, a tall man in a dingy raincoat, led me into the bathroom where he advised, "Tell me about this girl and what your friend did, then we will go and you won't have to see us again."

What could I tell them when I had no knowledge of what they wanted to know? I racked my brain to think of something that I could say to make them stop all this questioning but the only thing that came out of my mouth was, "I don't know anything, this is all a big surprise to me." At that point the short man came into the bathroom and shouted angrily, "I've had enough of this, we'll take them both to the Station." With that they hustled me through to the bedroom and said, "We are arresting both of you now!" This scared me and I begged Vincent, "Please what's this all about, tell them that I don't know what happened to any girl." He was too busy shouting and wearing at the men and ignored me. Then we were down the stairs and into a police car and on the way to Tooting Police Station where we were separated. I was put into a dirty bare room with walls covered in graffiti and left to wait for what seemed like hours before two other plain clothes men came into the room. Again it was the same question, "Why don't you tell us what was going on?

It will be better for you and everything will be over quickly." I wished that I did know something, they might have let me go home if I had something to tell them but I could only say that I didn't understand; I prayed for them to let me go. The two men withdrew to a corner of the room and whispered together, staring at me with such a menacing manner that I thought that they were planning to rape me; I felt so vulnerable and under their control. I concentrated my thoughts on the fact that I would soon be back at home. I was sure they would let me go home sometime that night, after all I hadn't done anything wrong. But somehow, unbelievably to me, I was later on taken to another room where a uniformed officer told me that I was charged with assisting in performing an illegal abortion. When I said that I hadn't done any such thing he told me to shut up as all the stuff had been found in my wardrobe. Then I was taken away and put into a cell that seemed to be deep underground like a catacomb. It was very cold and very uncomfortable; I was very frightened and feeling very low and confused. For some weeks I had been taking Valium, anyone who has tried to get off Valium will know how I felt to be suddenly cut off when I didn't want to be, especially in those circumstances. A police officer came into the cell and asked me for my belt and tie and I asked him if I could see a doctor but he just said, "In the morning" as he slammed the cell door shut and then I was alone. For a while I paced the floor but feeling myself getting panicky, I decided lie down on the rubber mattress and try to sleep but I could hear Vincent shouting and banging the steel lavatory door in his cell, he kept up the noise throughout the night but I eventually fell asleep exhausted.

The next morning the cell door opened and I was handed a disposable cup of tea and one piece of bread. The tea was foul and the bread revolting, it tasted damp and the meagre scrape of margarine must have been designed to taste especially bad, it couldn't have been made that way by accident. Shortly afterwards I was taken from the cell and joined Vincent and a motley crew of other men. We were taken in a Black Maria to the Magistrates Court in Ballham. There we were put together in another cold underground cell. I thought that now perhaps I could start to make sense of what had happened, I asked Vincent what was going on but he only told me not to worry, it will be all right and you will soon be out of here. We were then joined by Barry who seemed surprised to see me. Vincent told him that he should tell the police that I was not involved in anything. Barry did not answer, he didn't want to talk at all. I asked him "Barry what is going on, what have you two been up to? Please help me!" Barry didn't answer me either.

It soon became apparent why, as soon as we went into

court Vincent and I were put into the box but Barry was in the body of the court with his parents. Vincent and I had to stand and the charge was called out by the Clerk of the Court who asked us how we pleaded.

Vincent said firmly "Not Guilty and I said "Not Guilty".

Barry wasn't charged or asked to plead, he was going to give evidence against us for the police. We were not allowed to have bail as the police said that we would intimidate witnesses. I said that I didn't know any witnesses or what it was about anyway. Nobody listened to me, it was a frightening experience. The police had complete control of the proceedings and the court that day. We had nobody to represent us and the court mostly proceeded as if we weren't even there.

We were taken back to the cell, which was very cold. During the day we were given one sandwich with a nameless filling and some more tea as a midday meal.

Vincent and I waited together, without speaking, in that cold cell until the late afternoon when we were taken in that claustrophobic Black Maria to Brixton Prison.

The confined space in the Black Maria and the sound of the prison gates closing for the first time is something never to forget. Once inside the prison we were shepherded along long corridors to a room where we were asked questions regarding name, age, colour of eyes, next of kin and our fingerprints and photographs were taken. It was as if we were being taken into another dimension. Next we had to stand in line with the rest of the day's intake of men to be examined by the Doctor. I was cold and frightened, my heart was pounding. "Doctor, I have been taking Valium for the last two weeks, I need some help," I asked him. The Doctor, after the quickest examination possible said to the warder who accompanied him, "Give him two spoonfuls of the mixture." 'The Mixture' was a bottle of water with some aspirin roughly chopped up and half dissolved. This was the extent of the examination.

We were issued with a shirt and trousers to wear inside the prison, our own clothes and small personal possessions were listed and put into large brown paper bags. I liked the shirt, which was heavy cotton, white with a thin pale blue stripe. After that we were passed on to the bathhouse where we were to bathe.

After being alone the previous night and the long stay in that cold dirty cell in Tooting it was a needed relief to hear the sounds of other people talking and feel the warmth of the large bathhouse and the splash of the water. Lots of lovely hot water, I stood up to soap myself properly without thinking about the low dividing partitions between the tubs, immediately a guard rushed up and told me to sit down as everyone was going to look at me and he "Had enough problems thank you."

After this we were put into a large room to await our allocation to cells for the night,

We had more tea and bread, but most important was the comradeship that we suddenly found as we were all left alone in this room without supervision and could talk freely. At least the others did, I just sat there amazed. Here in this room were so many faces that I had seen in the newspapers that I had never thought to meet up with. There was a Doctor accused of killing several people, confidence men, shotgun robbers and there were also several men who wanted to talk to me and ask me questions but Vincent sat very close and answered for me, leaving no room for anyone to doubt who was in charge as far as I was concerned.

Somehow we were both put into the same cell. This at least was some comfort although we didn't talk much, I didn't know what to ask him. We talked about the flat and what would happen with the furniture and clothes etc. Vincent said, "When we have seen a lawyer we will get bail and it will be all right."

James, our landlord, was a qualified barrister although through the restrictions of the hidden racial barrier was not practicing but working as a nurse. He quickly got in touch with a firm of solicitors and the next morning he came with the lawyer and a barrister to see us. They all agreed that it would be easy for us to get bail when we next went to court, which was about a week away. At that time both they and I thought that it had only been one girl involved. Oh dear, what a mistake.

When the police started to investigate further and go through Vincent's address book they found dozens of girls that they were able to coerce into giving evidence against him. The mostly told the girls that someone had died, this made them very willing to co-operate. Consequently it wasn't so easy to get bail as it might have been, each time we went back to court the police mentioned new charges and more girls. The days in the prison passed very slowly, the one good thing was that there was a small library and men with people on the outside who visited them were kept supplied with newspapers and books, which I was able to read. Usually when we returned from our weekly visit to the Magistrates Court we managed to be put into the same cell and on the few occasions we were separated

Vincent always managed to get someone moved and me moved back in with him. I did spend nearly a whole week on another floor in a cell on my own and then I only saw him when we had our twice daily exercise which was a walk around the prison yard. We all went round and around until brought in. During these exercise walks several men approached me and asked if I would like to share their cell, I said no thank you, I had no wish to start a fight inside there! While I was on the fourth floor on my own there was a man who had helped the Doctor disposing of his victims, he was such a macho man with a threatening manner that somehow the warder in charge of that floor left his cell door open all day and at his request left mine open as well. I spent the long days with this man in his cell while he boasted of his exploits outside and showed me pictures of his latest boyfriend. I had to keep that friendship from Vincent, he wouldn't have believed it was so innocent on my part.

From that floor it is possible to see the Windmill, which is at the back of Brixton Hill, I kept looking at the windmill and wishing that I was outside in the fresh air and free to walk as I pleased. Hilda was sent to visit me on behalf of the Inspector and staff, she came about three times a week and was always at the Magistrates Court when we appeared there. She brought mints, chocolates and newspapers with her and was a most welcome visitor for me. The police questioned me every week and each time had new names to ask about, each time they asked me the names were unknown to me and I didn't have to lie to them at all – although they were convinced that I was lying. While going through Vincent's address book the police had been surprised at the types of people he had been mixing with. Politicians, society types and one or two titles. Vincent was a complete snob and loved to mix with those types of people.

I don't know how they thought he made the money which he must have spent but they undoubtedly knew after the police had contacted them. One of the detectives on the case that I met some years later told me that they were all surprised at the people Vincent knew and how frustrated they were at the support he had from some of the people they contacted. They hadn't realised that it was possible for a black person to move in those circles. I suppose Vincent was like the Krays in that aspect of his life. These brothers who we met inside Brixton Prison were, as is often told, perfect natural gentlemen and I wished that I had met them before. They both treated the warders with respect and their fellow prisoners they treated with solicitude and kindness.

The police opposed bail strenuously. When we first went before the Magistrate to ask for bail it was the same Magistrate that had dealt with the case we had against the Elcocks and he recognised us and told the court how and why he had seen us before.

He obviously was aware that the circumstances in which we were living were different to the police version where they tried to say we were together simply in order to do abortions. Our joint bank account book was produced as proof that we were doing this business together but as there was no money in the account and only showed minor usage that didn't hold up and eventually the Magistrate gave me bail on my own recognisance. If the police had been more honest at that time I know that he would have dismissed the case against me right there and then.

Vincent was refused bail again, by that time there were about twenty different charges of abortion against him and they included me as a conspirator. I went home that night and relaxed for the first time in two months. Ralf was overjoyed to see me in the kitchen once again. His friend had come from Hamburg to stay with him and they had bought a chicken and were wondering just how to cook it and here was Peter in the nick of time. I was so pleased to be out of the prison that I would have worked in the kitchen all day and night. I cleaned and seasoned the chicken and roasted it, we ate well that night and drank lots of wine and beers. My thoughts that Vincent was still stuck in that place made me cry. They tried to cheer me up by saying that it would not be long but when I enlightened them about the number of charges they realised why I was so glum. Ralf said, "I had no idea Vincent was doing anything like that". I said, "Well if I didn't know, how could you be expected to know."

They were collecting evidence against Vincent at a rate and he was refused bail until he appealed to the Judge in Chambers and by writing a letter to the Judge himself. He must have struck a cord with the Judge who allowed him bail but said that he must have three securities. By this time many of the Guyanese and certainly all his family with the exception of Ruth had deserted him. His sister who lived in North London did not contact him for years and he never forgave her for that; one particular cousin who I had thought was a very good friend and someone whom I could trust just disappeared from our lives the minute the police contacted her. We had a good Jamaican friend Ina who went to see the same cousin and his sister on Vincent's behalf, Ina made the journey across London with such good intentions but they were not pleased to see her and didn't even ask her to sit down. Ina was most upset by this but mostly concerned that family could treat family so badly. When I got my own bail I wrote to Vincent's mother in Guyana and to try to allay her fears I told her it was only a minor charge and that he wouldn't be in prison for long. I also told her about her daughter and the cousin but she replied that she wasn't surprised and that I should not worry but leave them to God and he will deal with them. After that we corresponded regularly and she addressed me as her son and signed her letters 'Moma' as she did to all her children.

I didn't know what to do about Vincent's bail. Ralf, as a foreigner, couldn't do it.

Hilda was willing but she wasn't a house owner, another colleague had been willing but her husband said no after the police had paid them a visit and told them that they were certain we would both leave the country as soon as Vincent was out on bail. I did not know at the time that a couple from Barbados who when they were first interviewed by the police their first question had been about the question of bail. "Shall we come to the station and bail them?" The police had told them that if they did stand bail for us we would both skip bail and then they would lose their house. They had retorted "If that is so, good let them do it and we will lose the house gladly." This of course did not endear them to the police who ignored them after that, especially when the wife went to great lengths explaining that her connection with us was mainly that I made hats for her and that we baked cakes for her and her friends. When I asked them if they would mind standing bail for Vincent they jumped at the chance to help. I asked Ina who had known us for some years since we had made her daughter's wedding cake. She was incensed at the attitude of the police and did not need asking twice. For the third bailee I asked Carl, a Grenadian friend. He had just bought his house and was also happy to do it. They all went to the police station late in the afternoon and then went to Brixton Prison to get Vincent. They were all so helpful and kind but I always felt it was shameful that no fellow Guyanese and in particular no relatives felt that they were able to help.

In spite of this Vincent never lost his high regard for his country and his mother suggested he 'left them to God'. As well as having to have three bailees Vincent also had to report to the police station once a day. This seemed to us a spiteful and unnecessary restriction as he had no intention of leaving England.

Before Vincent was given bail I visited the prison every day and took food for him.

On remand before trial you were allowed to receive papers, a meal, cigarettes and even a bottle of wine. I took everything, every day – even cigarettes because although he didn't smoke I felt sure they would be useful to him as 'currency'.

Vincent made friends with another South American, a man from Uruguay who was in prison charged with fraud and bigamy. Daniel's 'wife' was Spanish, very proper and very jealous. Carmelita gave me money twice a week so that I could cook and carry food in for her 'husband'. She was generous and gave me enough money to provide food for Vincent as well, I did it in style. Every day I got up early and cooked a variety of foods; I roasted chicken halves, pork chops, steak and fish. I baked all kinds of cakes and presented them as desserts with pots of cream and lots of fresh fruit. Visiting the prison became my focal point, as well as seeing Vincent there were the other 'wives'. Sometimes two wives would visit the same man and there would be a big fight in the waiting room. The wives and girlfriends were a mixed bunch, there were quiet frightened women and glamorous blondes who complained bitterly about their lowered standard of living while their man was inside. I heard tales of shotguns hidden in sheds and wardrobes and inside bedding, pedigree dogs, villas and expensive holidays; these were the women who dressed well when visiting. But the most famous mother and the most kind and sensitive visitor that I met was Mrs. Kray, Violet as she asked me to call her. She adored her sons and was equally kind and concerned about others. She questioned me about who I was visiting and consoled me. She asked me to introduce her to Vincent which I did, difficult though it was in those little cubicles and she waved a greeting to him as she passed whenever our visits coincided. The 'twins' made a point of talking to Vincent inside the prison, offering him sweets and kind words.

Dolly Kray, the wife of the twins' brother Charles was a visitor with her children and she had many kind words of encouragement to say to me. I think as always people liked the fact that Vincent was black and I was white and the openness with which I referred to him. The newspapers at the time were full of the Kray trial.

It seemed strange to read the things that were being

printed and I couldn't connect those things with the family that I had met who behaved so differently and had such obvious concern for others.

The man from Uruguay, Daniel, was connected with another family, the Richardsons, in the night club in Balham. Daniel had hit on a scheme of using the clubs plastic chip maker to forge the chips from other clubs and cash them in. This would have worked if Carmelita hadn't been so jealous and if she hadn't found out that he had been married twice before with no divorces. In her rage she told the police everything although once he had been arrested she was sorry but the damage had been done. Hell has no fury as they say.

I had found while in prison that many of the men were anxious to become friends with me, but while I was in Brixton I had no thoughts of sex even with Vincent when we were in a cell alone together I just couldn't stand the thought of it. But while I was out on bail and waiting for Vincent to get bail I got very lonely. While going to Brixton I had become friendly with another young man, Bob, who visited his friend in the prison and on one Saturday morning after visiting our respective friends we decided that we would go to the Vauxhall Tavern for a drink. There I met a very rough character called Leo. Leo was a Scot, his face covered with scars and he looked very hard and mean. Bob and I were sitting up at the long bar that curved down the middle of the pub where at night the drag queens would parade and dance and twist around the poles that rose from the bar to the ceiling. Bob and I were talking, mainly about our friends' cases, I think Bob's friend had been charged with some kind of fraud or theft. While talking I twisted around on my stool and saw Leo. He frowned at me and I immediately turned away, thinking how mean he looked. The crowd in the Vauxhall on Saturday mornings was more mixed than in the evenings and I thought he might resent my looking at him.

In the reflection of the mirror behind the bar I could see Leo coming towards us.

I thought my God he is going to bash me for looking at him. As he came nearer I quailed in my shoes. He leant over my shoulder and placed a pound note on the bar.

"Get yourself a drink," he said roughly and then he was gone back to stand against the wall on the far side. I breathed again, got my drink and when I turned to thank him he came over and said that he would take me to lunch. It was not a question it was a statement. When the pub closed at three o'clock we stayed on and drank, there was no question of anyone asking Leo to leave before he was ready to go. I never did find out exactly what he did but no-one in any of the bars we went to dared to upset him. When we eventually left the Vauxhall of five o'clock a car and driver was waiting for him outside, we went to 'lunch' and ate fillet steaks with a bottle of wine. Afterwards he said, "Let's go to your place Peter." I said no, I still didn't know just what I had let myself in for and knew that Ralf would be there and maybe no understand or rather understand too well and resent it. In any case it didn't seem the right time to take Leo there. He took me to a bed and breakfast house somewhere in Camberwell that he said was known as 'The Snake pit'.

His driver waited for us outside while we went in and Leo booked a room.

He also paid £4 for two cups of coffee and in 1968 that was a lot of money; however he had a large roll of notes and money didn't seem to matter much to him.

Once we were in the room alone he became very loving and quite unlike the impression given by his face and his behaviour in public. He made love to me four times that afternoon, he told me that he had never made love more than once a day before and that if ever I had to go to prison I shouldn't worry because I would want for nothing inside "Peter, all the Mars bars you can eat, I promise you."

Although the room we occupied overlooked the street he didn't bother to go out of the room to go to the bathroom but just opened the window and pissed over the the windowsill. I said you can't do that and he answered, "I always do it, I've paid enough for this room they won't bother about that even if they notice."

We left Camberwell about eight o'clock and they drove mc home to Streatham.

Ralf saw me get out of the car and asked, "Who was that?" I answered, "Just a cousin," the way that Vincent did when questioned about a new friend. Then a week later while I was watching television on my own I heard a loud banging on the front door. I started down the stairs but Harold, James' cousin had already opened it.

Harold was confused; Leo was there, his face and fists covered in blood trying to explain who it was he wanted, "Couldn't remember your name," said Leo, "But I remembered the house and I needed to see you, where can I wash?" No wonder Harold looked shocked – to have a stranger appear at the door in that state and asking for someone whose name he didn't know would shock anyone. Only the fact that Leo was white made him think that it was me that Leo wanted. When Leo had washed I wanted to bathe his cuts with antiseptic but he wouldn't hear of it, when I asked him what had happened he just said, "Some problem, all taken care of now" and that was all he would say. I made a meal for Leo and his driver and afterwards we went out for a drink, after that he came regularly to the house at about four o'clock in the afternoon. His driver would sit drinking coffee while Leo plied me with gin and chocolates. Then when I was dressed to suit him we would all make a round of the South London pubs. He delighted in Irish pubs where he would pull the wires out of the juke box if they played Irish tunes. Somehow no one made any effort to control him, certainly not me. His pockets were full of change, he only used notes to pay for anything, maybe the notes were false, I don't know if they were and I didn't ask him what he did for a living, I had seen and heard too much in Brixton Prison to go into that. After all I felt that it was possible that I might go to prison for something that I knew nothing about so I thought I would get used to being a 'Gangsters Moll' as I would probably end up like that anyway. Leo started to sleep with me every night, sending his driver home to return for him at 8am. Each morning Leo gave me money to buy his dinner, a handful of notes each time. With that money and the money I had from Carmelita I could afford to buy the best food in the shops and not worry about how much it cost. I bought fillet steaks and salmon regularly – only the best for Leo and my two boys in prison. Leo usually came back to the house at 4pm, after eating we made love and then got ready to go out. Each evening had the same routine, dozens of pubs in the South East where I had to drink light ale with a gin and tonic, with Leo there was no choice of drink, that is what he liked and that is what you had as well. Each night we finished up at the Vauxhall Tavern where Leo would go into the public bar and send drinks to me in the bar with the drag queens. From the little conversation I heard in the public bar the men Leo talked with seemed to be interested in Antiques, currency exchange rates and properties abroad. When Leo had enough of this bar we would drive to the Embankment and park outside the steps to Villiers Street. A constant stream of young boys and men would come to the car to talk to Leo. I didn't know what about as I was busy queening it in the back of the car eating my chocolates and drinking beers. One Saturday Leo came back early in the day and left at 4pm saying that he had something on and should be back very late that night. I waited for him but he didn't come back and that was the last I saw of him. Maybe he was arrested, I didn't know. I met Violet and Reggie's girlfriend Carol near the Old Bailey one morning when I had been to see the barrister who was to represent me at the trial.

We went for coffee and toast and the A.B.C. opposite. Mrs. Kray was so sure that the twins would be released and she talked of her plans for them when they came home. While talking to Carol I casually put Leo's name into the conversation but she didn't know him. Looking back why should she know him even if he had been involved with the twins, after all Vincent was being charged and I knew nothing about his affairs. Mixing with the visitors at Brixton changed my ideas. After all wasn't I out on bail being charged with something I knew nothing about. It gives one sympathy for others who claim to be in the same position, whereas before I might have assumed they were lying. Soon after the episode with Leo, Vincent was out on bail and I had that to think about. I was worried each day until I knew that he had reported to the police station.

Once the trial started Vincent was taken back into custody but I was allowed to go home each night and report back to the Old Bailey each morning. During the day I had to stay inside the Old Bailey and as I had to wait in a cell until it was time to go into court I wondered if this was how I would end up. Each morning on the way in I arranged for a meal to be sent in for Vincent together with a clean shirt each day.

I was anxious that he eat something nice for as long as possible and I also wanted him to feel as well as I could make him. I was awake very early each morning, I feared that I might oversleep and be late for the court and they might make me stay there overnight and I wanted to be at home so that if Vincent needed me to do anything I would be able to do so. Although I had some misgivings about Vincent's behaviour regarding my part in the case and we had reached a difficult point in our relationship as he was being so blatantly unfaithful to me. I still could not turn my back on him at all, it had become as if he was a part of me that I could not deny. The trial at the Old Bailey lasted for seven days. Each day I stood in the dock with Vincent listening to the evidence against him. There was a stream of young women that passed through the witness box Luckily none of them knew me, even the ones that I had seen didn't remember me, moreover none of them could remember seeing a white person at the flat except Barry. The prosecution tried very hard to prove a connection between myself and the women but their puzzled glances at me in the dock confirmed to everyone present that they didn't know me and were wondering just why I was there.

The visitors gallery was full each day and I was supported there by Hilda from the Inspector of Taxes. The Inspector sent her each day to report back to him and give me any support that I might need, this was the kindly face of the Revenue and for which I was grateful; also every day came Kenneth, Sugar's husband who had helped to get Vincent out on bail. We sat in the dock while the witnesses gave their evidence, each day was a monologue of Vincent's affairs. I was shocked at so many Guyanese that came to give evidence against him. Even people unconnected with the abortions were called in to give discrediting testimony about his character. Some of them he didn't even know. There is nothing like a star down on their luck for the vultures of envy to gather. A postman who claimed relationship to Vincent was one of the few men called. His evidence was given so piously as if Vincent had forced him to have unprotected sex with a young girl. He was like a rabbit afraid of a weasel, bobbing in front of the court like a frightened slave in a movie. All the evidence pointed to the fact that Vincent had performed the abortions with the utmost discretion and care. All his patients had received antibiotics and good aftercare from him. The method he used (insertion of a slim tube) to produce a somewhat natural type of miscarriage would later be used legally by nursing homes after the law had been changed to allow abortions. He was a man ahead of his time. When I went into the witness box to give evidence the prosecution tried to give the impression that I had assisted or co-operated in the abortions. Pointing to the equipment laid out on the table in front of the Judge, the prosecutor asked the jury, "How could Simpson see all this and not know or ask what it was for?" 'All this' included the speculum that must have come from Guyana in 1965, various syringes and boxes of penicillin and pieces of rubber tubing. When asked by my counsel the prosecution agreed that it had all been in the old carrier bag hidden at the bottom of the wardrobe and as the pictures of the bedroom handed to the jury showed, the room was in complete confusion. The faces of the jury showed that they wouldn't have known what it was either, so they were all confident that I hadn't known anything about it.

The prosecution tried to keep the impression going that I had been merely a friend or business partner but my counsel who like the counsel in our previous encounter with the law had advised me not to be shy of words gently led me and I told the Jury just how much I loved Vincent and how jealous I had been of Barry who I thought was having a passionate affair with Vincent. Barry had been asked about taking drugs when he gave his evidence against Vincent. He had been taken aback by the question but had to agree that he was a drug user. Barry who gave his evidence in a shuffly shifty manner was later convicted of stealing cars and imprisoned. When I read about it I felt as if some kind of justice had been done to him. I made sure that there was no doubt of my disapproval of both drugs and abortions and after my evidence not one person in the court was unsure of me. Here was I a man who openly loved another man and because of that I was on trial. I'm sure that the colour combination again was so unexpected at that time and the poignancy of it did not escape notice. Vincent was found guilty on some but not all the charges against him and sentenced to three years but I was found not guilty on any charge and released immediately. When I emerged through the doors at the rear of the courtroom the entire jury was waiting for me, they were so kind and both the women and the men wanted to cuddle and kiss me and wish me good luck.

In another court at the Old Bailey the Kray twins had been on trial and I found myself behind the cells waiting to visit Vincent along with Dolly, Violet and Carol and some of the other wives I had met at Brixton prison. In spite of their own concerns the Kray women all put their arms around me and tried to comfort me saying that a three-year sentence would soon pass and that Vincent would be all right. We weren't allowed to stay very long; it was a miserable hurried visit but outside Hilda and Kenneth were waiting to take me home. Two weeks later I received a letter from the Inspector inviting me back to work. Apparently the head office had advised against this, but the Inspector had taken a poll of his staff and they were all adamant that I should return to the office. After all I had done nothing wrong and had no record to impede me. This had a double impact on me as the rest of the staff were quite prejudiced at that time and I had thought not particularly aware. However, they, without exception, welcomed me with open arms, concerned very much about Vincent and assuring me that the time would soon pass and we would be together again. I didn't mention my feelings to anyone but at that time I wasn't so sure if I wanted to be 'back together again'. Vincent had not really been very protective as far as I was concerned, he had tried to protect himself firstly by saying that the wardrobe with all his equipment in was mine and then by asking me to conceal the fact that we were lovers. If I had tried to do this and denied that I was gay it would have seemed as if I had something to hide after all and had indeed been a part of the abortion business. If I had done what he asked I would probably been imprisoned. Because of Vincent's activities I had been put at risk from the law, he had never told me what he was doing. Not the least of it, he had been spending a lot of money on drinks and socialising at times when I had been worrying about how to pay our bills. I told myself that if I met someone else to live with I would not see him when he came out of prison. But no matter how much I went out and how many men I met I still felt a sense of loss all the time and longed for him to be home.

CHAPTER NINE.

The time between visits seemed to grow longer each month. Vincent was sent to Maidstone prison where he remade contact with Daniel, but he wrote heartrending letters to me that filled me with despair. Each time he wrote those desperate letters I telephoned Violet who in spite of her own sadness comforted me and laughed at her own problems with the twins who were imprisoned at opposite ends of the country so that she had two long journeys to make when she visited them. I don't know why they did that but it didn't seem right to me that such a devoted mother should have to cope with that situation. But at least the authorities were kind to us and eventually transferred Vincent back to London to Wormwood Scrubs, which was easier to get to and the fare not so expensive. Wormwood Scrubs had a harsh appearance, the prisoners all had a different downhearted look and came into the visiting room very cautiously as if expecting to be rebuffed. On visiting days I prepared myself with a miniature vodka to put in the tea that we were allowed to purchase so that Vincent could have a drink. A Valium so that he could get over the let down feeling after the visit and a pound note or a five pound note wrapped tightly in tin foil so that he could conceal it in his mouth. I had no idea what or how he could use the money but I felt that he would put it to his advantage.

Although I was now to all intents technically free and single, I didn't feel single.

I still did everything that we always did and after some brief flirtations just went to work, watched television and waited for the months to pass. Before Vincent was bailed I had taken most of our furniture up to Wivenhoe and arranged to let the maisonette through an agent so that the mortgage would be paid even if I was not free. James helped me to change the sitting room into a bed sitting room and I kept the kitchen, James took back the other rooms and reduced the rent for me. James was like Vincent in some ways. The telephone rang constantly as his girl friends tried to contact him, but James was mostly a 'love and leave' lover. Only the most dedicated women could hold his attention for long. After one spectacular fight on the doorstep between two of them, his wife Lynette just walked out and never came back.

She just left with the clothes she was wearing, all her ornaments, shoes, dresses, everything, she just left it all behind. James was devastated; it is one thing to be unfaithful to your wife but another thing to lose her. In less than two weeks though one lady had installed herself in his bed and was warning off all the other contenders.

This lady was tough, she had a small shop in Balham market selling cottons, buttons and zips. She accepted commissions to make wedding dresses, but from the number of irate women calling at the house she had no satisfied customers. This didn't deter her and when they called at the house to complain she just abused them, sometimes reducing the unfortunate woman to tears. Ralf finished his term at Merrill Lynch and left to go to New York for a year. I was very unsettled in the house and Edna, one of Vincent's many cousins, who lived two streets away encouraged me to rent the top half of a house she had bought in Earlsfield. She promised to charge me the same rent for four rooms as James was charging me for two rooms. With help from Kenneth I moved over to Earlsfield. At first I liked it there but it was a bit isolated compared to Streatham. Luckily the family that rented the bottom flat were very friendly to me and Cherry, who made curtains for a living encouraged me to sew.

She taught me the difficult art of sewing curtains and I went some days to Chelsea to Carmelita to learn how to make and sew women's clothes. This way the long months passed and after a year Vincent was eligible for parole. A social worker came to see where he would be living. I showed him the spare bedroom, which I told him would be Vincent's room in case he had any prejudices about two men living together.

Everything went well and Vincent was granted his parole. I was excited that morning going to meet Vincent at Wormwood Scrubs and arrived there about an hour before he came out. Vincent came out with so many things we really needed a small van to carry them. I knew that he had plenty of books that had been sent in for him but I was unprepared for the paintings that he said he had done but which I think had been given to him. We came home on the bus and I thought that he would like to be able to see everything but he complained that we hadn't taken a taxi. I couldn't afford that but it would have been easier considering the amount of belongings he had managed to accumulate. When we got to Earlsfield I could see that he wasn't pleased with where we were living, Cherry greeted him but he hardly acknowledged her. I did assume that would spend at least the first night together so that we could talk but the Dutchman Jan came in the late afternoon and took Vincent out to the theatre. I wasn't even mentioned in their plans and spent the evening in front of the television alone, realising that nothing had changed.

I had taken the mortgage for the maisonette from the G.L.C. and after they had paid a visit to Wivenhoe and realised that I had a tenant they wrote to me and insisted that I did not lease out the property. In order to pay the mortgage I took a Saturday job in a gent's outfitter in Kingston. The basic wage was around two pounds ten shillings – but with commission added I earned at least five pounds each Saturday. This was just enough to pay the mortgage. As a Saturday salesman I came lowest in the serving order. First was the Head Salesman, then the other full time staff and last of all me unless I had already served the customer before. I soon developed a technique of 'recognising' people as they came in the door.

"How good to see you again," I would say brightly as if I knew them, "You're looking well" and then guiding them into the body of the shop where I would start talking quickly to give the impression to the other salesmen that this was either a friend or one of my regular customers. The customers were bemused by this and some of them asked me where we had met before, but they didn't object to the warm welcome and it enabled me to steal them away from the other salesmen. One of the full time staff was a young man who hoped to manage a shop further into the stock broker belt. He was extremely well educated but not very articulate and a little slow.

I 'helped' him to finish off his sales and sneaked my initials onto his sales slips so that the commission came to me. My speciality in selling was to push suits that had been made to measure but not collected, there was double commission on those, I arranged for alterations that I knew would not be suitable when they were finished but none of my customers came back to complain, I got one young man into a suit that had been made for a six footer and he was barely five feet. I met him years later and he told me that it was the best suit he had ever bought, maybe he liked buying it from me.

This work was exhilarating but tiring and I knew I wouldn't be able to keep up that pace indefinitely. The Post Office were advertising heavily for staff. Engineers were being offered the best wages but had to have technical qualifications. Nearly as good were the wages for Telegraphists, much more than I could earn as a Clerical Assistant for the Inspector of Taxes, even after they increased our wages as we had been getting 'below poverty' rates. I applied for a position as a Telegraphist and had the good luck to meet an extremely nice man at the interview who made the more or less filled in the application for me; when he took me to the typing room for my typing test I just had to show him the type of machine I had at home and that was enough. On the first day that I reported for training we all had to meet next to the model of a cable laying ship in the foyer of Electra

House, a large building on the Victoria Embankment next to the Thames. The first person I saw was Doreen who had been Willy's lover and standing close by her a tall friendly girl, Winsome, who was to become my closest friend in the Post Office. There was about twenty of us altogether but Doreen, Winsome and I stayed together and giggled our way through the first day. I was soon engulfed in a wave of learning. First we had to know how to compose a telegram for transmission abroad, we learnt to type on three bank keyboards and then go on to telex machines and finally after four years we were allowed to train on the keyboards that punched out the five-unit tape that actually sent messages abroad. Up until then we were only concerned with the telegrams that arrived in the U.K. for delivery and the receiving of messages on the telephone and telex machines from customers and Post Offices that we would prepare and hand to the Class 1 operators for transmission overseas. From relative poverty as a Clerical Assistant I was soon able to afford a holiday for Vincent and I. Most of us new telegraphists had come from poorly paid jobs, the difference after a few months, especially with the amount of overtime we all did, was obvious. We could now afford to buy the latest styles in clothing and talk about holidays, saving for a deposit on a house and buying jewellery. Some of the women from the Caribbean who had young children brought their elderly Aunts or Mothers over with the idea that they would look after the children and free them to do the maximum amount of overtime. This was a short-lived fashion as these elderly ladies soon made friends with other ladies who unveiled the secrets of getting money from the state via those nice payment books that were cashed at the Post Office and not only that, they learnt that it was possible to get a Council flat. These missions accomplished they soon left the daughter or niece and started a new life for themselves.

I suggested to Vincent that we go to Austria for a holiday, I had been there before and remembered it with affection and hoped that a holiday together would be a new beginning for us. At that time I wasn't keen on flying and it wasn't such a popular way to travel as it is nowadays. We went on the train to Dover and caught the ferry across the channel to Ostend where we boarded the train to go across Belgium and Germany reaching Vienna early the next morning. We both enjoyed Vienna, I had booked the pension before leaving home. I think they were a little surprised to see Vincent and he certainly attracted a lot of attention. They were intrigued by the was he dressed, he had taken all his suits with him and appeared at all the meal times fully suited, his fingers shone with his rings and he behaved imperiously refusing to speak even one word of German. He had a habit when he needed to ask a question of saying, "Do you speak English?" and if the answer was "Nein" or "Sorry" he would dismiss them pre-emptorily with a wave of his hand as if dismissing a wayward servant. But Vienna had something for both of us, we visited all the tourist attractions like the Schonenburg Palace where he took pictures of me in which I never appeared, he just aimed the camera and hoped for the best. I gorged myself on the exquisite chocolate cake with cream and the luxurious chocolates while Vincent made the most of their savoury dishes – the small pickled fishes served on rolls all over the place were his favourite and the cold white wine that was served everywhere from early morning was a hit with both of us. We were booked at the pension for one week and as we were so near to Hungary we decided to spend a week there. It looked close on the map but actually took a day travelling in the train. In our carriage was a couple who had been on their honeymoon in England, the man had bought his wife some gold rings and was worried that the border police might confiscate them, I think it was more to do with currency restrictions than anything else. Vincent took them from the man and put them in his pocket, the border police were very courteous to us all and there was no incident. The man gave us his telephone number and address and while we were in Budapest we visited them, they prepared gnocchi for us and we drank wine that they had brought from the father's house in the country. While in England and even in Vienna we had heard many tales of the hardship behind the iron curtain but we saw no evidence of that in Budapest. The couple we met on the train owned their own house, the shops were full of the latest fashions, the food shops had a plentiful selection of all kinds of foods and the people were fat! The September nights were warm, the shops were open late into the night and the streets were filled with men and women walking, sitting on benches in the parks talking easily, the women's handbags resting on the seats beside them with no fear that they would be stolen. In the 'free' Europe it would have been impossible to sit like that without being mugged. We went back to Vienna from Budapest and spent another three days there, just long enough for Vincent to go to the opera in his best black suit and for me to go to the funfair where I met a Viennese gentleman who took me out to a nightclub to eat and dance. The journey back to England seemed to go on forever. Firstly the train from Vienna was delayed for four hours and then late at night when we started, the arrangements for the sleepers were confused and we had to sit up all night in a cramped compartment. We travelled through Germany the next day but the castles

perched along the Danube River failed to arouse any interest to any of us on the train.

We reached Ostend with time to go to a restaurant before we had to board the ferry.

We relaxed and ate and drank quite a lot and started to feel better. Better that is until we got on board the ferry, the wind was blowing and it was raining heavily. The ferry pitched around before we started off and once underway went round and round like a corkscrew. I managed not to be sick only by sitting upright and keeping as still as possible. The poor man next to me had his wife to look after and later took on the case of Vincent who was being sick and groaning pitifully. I couldn't help him, I knew that if I tried I would be ill as well and I couldn't face it. I thought that we would never see the comfort of our own home again. When we did get home I fell into the front door gratefully, after a cup of English tea we went to bed and slept. We slept throughout the rest of the day and that night thankfully waking up refreshed the next morning. Before leaving for Austria we had invited the friends who had helped us during the trial to a celebration. Hilda and her son, Kenneth and Sugar, Ina and her latest handsome gentleman friend, Carl and Jasmine and Cherry and Holly from the flat downstairs. We had laughed, drank and ate until late and leaving the mess behind had gone on holiday. It now faced me on the morning after we returned but I didn't mind cleaning then, at least the floor didn't pitch and toss all over the place like that ferry had done. Vincent had been invited to the High Commissioner's residence in Lowndes Square to cook for an important dinner party they were giving for the Mayor of Washington. The High Commissioner, Sir John Carter was so impressed that he suggested that Vincent should work for them. Vincent became their Butler and supervised the kitchen staff. The position suited Vincent in that it was a small household and he fitted in well when the Carters entertained.

Sir John's wife, Sara-Lou, was an exotic, creamy coloured Southern American belle, who gathered around her a circle of sparkling young people, dancers, actors, personalities, the wives of all the other High Commissioners and the wives of wealthy Americans living in London. At least once a month Sara-Lou presided over a fashion show or entertainment in aid of charity. These were happy days for Vincent and happy days for me as well to know that he was working in an acceptable way.

The one thing Vincent wasn't happy about was living in Earlsfield and then his cousin Edna asked us to pay much more rent. When we said no she tried to say that she wanted to live there and that we would have to leave anyway. I went to the fair rent tribunal and they not only gave us security of tenure but they made the rent more than half of what we had been paying and back dated it so that we lived for months without paying any rent. I was so pleased that I went to the Gas Board and bought a new stove with an oven big enough to bake six large cakes at once. It wasn't pleasant living there after that though and Vincent went to Streatham to talk to James who was happy to think that we might return there to live. James was preparing to leave London to live in Jamaica, not with the woman who had been there before but to another very pretty woman who he intended to marry when Lynette had completed her divorce proceedings. While James was preparing to go, the Balham Market lady let herself in with her key and removed every scrap of his furniture. Left with an empty house James asked us to take over the whole place, which we did and later we agreed to buy the house from him. It took some time but I sold the maisonette in Wivenhoe and borrowed one thousand pounds from Winsome to have enough to put down as a deposit. At that time not many Building Societies were willing to give a mortgage to two men but Nationwide gave us a mortgage without misgivings. These upheavals gave Vincent the opportunity to decide that he had better give up his job with the High Commissioner and stay at home where he could, "Concentrate on my cakes and catering." Being at home all day, gradually the fair-weather friends and relatives crept back into the limelight of Vincent. No-one that knew him could resist him and stay away from him too long. He was a natural healer and like a sin eater of the old days. Men and women would come to him and unburden their problems leaving him exhausted with the secrets that they told him. They were secure in the knowledge that he wouldn't repeat their confidences. This had been proved at the trial when he had implicated nobody although he could have named many, even from the highest spheres of Guyana society. This of course is not to say that he was above using this knowledge to benefit himself whenever he needed a favour or someone to help him when he, as usual, left large catering jobs until the last minute.

But for me he was miraculous, whenever I had an ache or pain I would tell him and it needed a touch from him to cure it. He knew that he had this gift but he told me, "After all that other business I don't want to have anything to do with any kind of medicine." What he really liked to do was to talk about his family. He could trace the family tree back through the generations to England and Scotland, what was said when his Great Grandparents met and he knew all the branches of his family. He had a brain like a computer file keeping every scrap of information ready to be pulled out at a moments notice. Years later a neighbour in Clapham High Street told me, "I tell him something once and that together with what my other family members tell him is enough for him to build up a complete history of my family." Myself, never close to my own family got to know more about his family and Guyana than I ever knew of my own family or England. Over the years we were together I heard so much talk about Guyana each day that when I finally got there for the first time it was as if I had been born there myself. I could recognise the streets and landmarks as if I'd seen them before. While in Georgetown I was continually asked, "How is it that you are so at home here?" and I did feel so completely at home. I always thought that it was the continuous talk about Guyana but now that I think about it more and remember that my Mother on first seeing Vincent had said how much he looked like my Father. When I first went to Skinningrove in Yorkshire I felt the same way, as if I belonged there. Maybe I did belong to both places, after all my Father had come from Guyana himself all those years ago. Vincent was so taken up with his own image of himself that although I took it for granted that everyone was aware of our relationship, especially after the trial, he often tried to disguise the facts telling local tradesmen that he was my brother-in-law. It seemed to be some desire on his part for some sort of social acceptance, not quite realising that our English society will accept certain things if they are part of a stable relationship which to all outwards appearances we were. Vincent spent more and more time outside the home. He went back to sleeping for most of the day while I was out at work. When I returned he was either getting ready to go out or already be out. He would offer no explanation of where he had been or with whom. I didn't object too strongly, a man will do what he wants to anyway, regardless of protests or arguments and I did encourage him to take a dominant role in our life, I wanted to live with a man not just a friend and his behaviour became part of that. I was concerned however that he might be tempted back into old practices. I searched the house regularly to make sure that there was nothing even vaguely medical hidden anywhere. We had a steady stream of wedding catering and working with such a huge number of people at Electra House I got some catering work from there. At first when we took over the house we let most of the spare rooms but gradually went over to doing bed and breakfast, a large part of this was due to Mohammed and Egyptian friend who introduced families from Egypt to us. Whenever we catered for a wedding it was Mohammed that supplied his friends as waiters for us. When those Arabs worked for us Vincent was constantly on duty, keeping a close watch on me in case I got too friendly with any of them. I had wanted to join an organisation call Gay Liberation but Vincent to me that I was liberated enough and I didn't need to join them. Ideally he liked me to go to work unshaven and return straight home to start my domestic chores. But much as I, in a way, liked this domination I was becoming disillusioned. Being left alone so much and not being able to invite anyone home without first consulting Vincent or risk the start of a jealous row, I began to feel that life was passing by and I was just standing still.

CHAPTER TEN.

In 1973 Vincent went to Hamburg to visit Ralf who was now working as a commodity broker, with a wife, a house in the country and a huge apartment in Hamburg. I understood that the idea of the visit was to finalise an idea of Ralf's to set Vincent up in a restaurant in Hamburg. Willingly I gave Vincent the money for the fare, anxious to see him settled in anything legitimate. I was quite prepared to go to Germany to live if necessary, however on his return from Hamburg he made no mention of any plans and when I asked him he ignored me. The restaurant story in Hamburg had been just that, a story concocted so that he could get the money to go on holiday. Shortly after his return from Hamburg he did start work again in a restaurant in Brompton Road. They employed a lot of Brazilians there and we soon had young Brazilian men calling him on the telephone making little secret assignations. Then one day I returned from work to find the front door broken and the house ransacked. Vincent said that this was a sign that he should have been at home and shortly after that stopped going out to work again. That winter was the start of the mineworkers bid to obtain more recognition and better conditions. I was in sympathy with them; my Grandfather had worked in the iron mine in Skinningrove, Yorkshire and my Mother had often told me of the hardships and total control the owners had over the miners. The government introduced a three-day week in order to conserve fuel but telegrams were considered essential and we worked as usual doing even more overtime. Power cuts meant that streets and houses were in darkness for hours during the day and at night. Hospitals were exempted from the cuts and as the house was near to Tooting Bec hospital we escaped the cuts. I would leave Tooting Bec underground and walk along the pitch dark streets and then turning the corner of the common there would be our house ablaze with lights like a beacon. Still in the effort to enlarge the cake making business I called on a photographer to take some pictures of cakes that we were making for a wedding. The photographer had a shop near Tooting Bec underground, he told us that he was not doing good business and wanted to leave. The lease was available for £1,000. Vincent went to see the shop and thought it could make a good restaurant, we borrowed £1,000 on a second mortgage from National Securities and started negotiations for the lease. After all that the photographer decided to stay, I put the money into our Nationwide savings account to that it could make some interest while we thought about something else to do. The months went by and no other opportunities arose. In Guyana, Vincent's parents were not so well. "Peter I could use some of the money and visit them, that is if you are willing." While telling me about his parents he looked close to tears and later his kind attentions to me made me agree that we should use some of the money. Vincent invited my Mother down from Yorkshire for a visit, "She will be company for you while I am away," he explained. In reality she would be an unwitting watchdog for him in case I had any ideas of entertaining someone whilst he was away.

Mother came down from Yorkshire a week before he left, I took some days leave that were owing to me so that we could spend more time together and go out on trips, it had been a long time since we spent so much time together and the weeks that Vincent was away passed quickly. While he was away I spring-cleaned the whole house but as soon as he returned it was a mess again. He brought a pair of Gold Creole earrings for my mother, which she loved, but nothing for me. Somehow he had managed to get thirteen bottles of rum through Customs without any difficulty which was nice; he also bought mangoes and a fruit called carambola, which is known in Guyana as five-finger and in England as star fruit. Chocolate to boil and drink and lots of hot pepper sauce and mango atchar. These small events filled my life without much sense of satisfaction, I was working long hours in order to keep up the payments on the house and on the second mortgage; by 1975 I had come to the conclusion that it was time that I make a stand for myself and when two of the men I worked with suggested a holiday I agreed. We went to Tenerife, that beautiful island in the Atlantic leaving Heathrow one grey February afternoon and by the next morning I was sitting outside in the hot sunshine drinking brandy and eating strawberries and cream. I pictured Vincent at home wondering what I was doing but for once I didn't care. For the first time in years I felt as if I was living a little part of life just for me.

Jim and Keith, my colleagues were great fun to be with and they had no hang ups about meeting people. We had taken a self-catering apartment for the three of us and on the second day we went to the Supermercade to buy some supplies. About half way around the shop Jim disappeared with a young man that just happened to pass by. Keith and I finished the shopping but by the time I reached outside with the bags he had disappeared as well. I went back to the apartment to find the door securely locked from the inside. I left the shopping outside the door and went downstairs to the bar, after about two hours I went back to the apartment and this time I could get in. Keith wasn't there but the shopping had been put away and the rooms tidied. Someone had cooked rice and a stew. When Keith came back three hours later I thanked him for putting away the groceries, "Oh it wasn't me, the boy with me did that and he cooked for us as well, I'm sorry about the door but he was shy." Not too shy for Keith I thought. Jim did not come back until the next day, he had been in the mountains he said with two Germans. His face was bruised and cut but he said that he had been involved in an accident as well as having his adventure. On that holiday I didn't have any adventures, I wasn't used to the freedom and felt inhibited as if Vincent was still in control. I kept busy enjoying the sights of Tenerife, the streets and parks were full of hot coloured flowers, vibrant reds and yellows and overlooking the whole island was the volcano with it's topping of snow. From the hotel window you could see banana plantations and growing in the hotel gardens were trees laden with oranges and grapefuit. When it was time to go home I cut down a large plastic water bottle and filled it with strawberries to take home to Vincent and some of the oranges with the leaves still attached but he didn't show any pleasure in them and for the next few weeks hardly talked to me at all except to make remarks about how selfish I was. We were very busy at work and I was able to do a lot of overtime and tried to keep out of his way so that we wouldn't fight. Doing so much overtime I was able to pay all the bills and still have some money left over to save. I thought that I would save the money for myself but there were soon demands on my savings. The roof leaked and had to be replaced so I paid for that. I worked very hard and saved again and the next February went to Gran Canaria with Jim. The island and the town of Las Palmas had a different atmosphere to Tenerife; there were lots of men from North Africa who were ready to flirt, making sexy suggestions when they approached in the streets. I succumbed while in a restaurant with Jim. We had gone to have our lunch at 12 noon and kept having 'just one more bottle of wine' until it was about 4 o'clock. A handsome young Moroccan asked if I had a light for his cigarette, the next moment he was sitting at our table talking to me as if we were the only ones there. "Come with me," he asked and when I asked him where he said that he knew of a nice hotel where we could be alone. It is not a good thing to meet someone when you have been drinking a lot of wine. By the time I realised my mistake it was nearly too late. The 'nice hotel' was like the Snakepit in Camberwell but its conditions made Camberwell a paradise by comparison. The room we were in had twin beds that looked as if no-one had actually slept in them but just laid on top of them, the pillows had the unmistakable signs of many greasy heads. Nothing happened between us in the room except that I was sick in the man's shoes, at first I felt humiliated by that but once out on the street I was pleased that I had done it. This nice young man suggested not only that I should pay the hotel bill but that I should give him some money as well. By the time he made his suggestion about money we were out on the street and I shouted loudly for all to hear, "Pay? Pay? what me? what for? you can't even fuck." All the while I was beating his head with my camera, he hadn't met anyone like me I'm sure and he ran off down a side street cringing with embarrassment. After that I was more careful when being approached by strangers no matter how nice they looked. I had always laughed at holiday romances and thought that it would never happen to me but it did. I suppose if I had been happier at home it might not have happened at all. For the first three days of our holiday a young man, always in the near distance, had followed me very shyly.

He appeared and smiled his shy smile through bars, shops and cafes but never coming close enough to speak to me. One night Jim and I were drinking at the bar in a café off the main square when he sat down beside me. He ordered his drink and shyly indicated that he wished to buy a drink for me, he spoke to the waiter who asked me what I would like to have. He was resplendent in a red jacket, preening himself in the male Spanish way, but hesitantly said, "Tu Dance?" "Si," I answered telling him my name was Peter, he didn't understand until I managed to say Pedro. "Ah Pedro, dance?" he smiled so sweetly that I was lost. By this time Jim had discretely disappeared so I didn't have to worry about him. We went dancing and drinking and although shy Manolo took control, this was a young Vincent in the making, I suppose that is the type I attract. Manolo guided me around the dance floors of Las Palmas and through all the bars where he was well known to all the bar staff. His pride in being with me was evident in the way he introduced me to all his friends and he insisted on paying for everything. This was pleasing to me as all the other tourists were paying for their friend's drinks and here was I being treated like a betrothed. Manolo spoke no English at all and I very little Spanish, we communicated that night through the bar staff and waiters who translated for me the "Te quiero" that Manolo kept whispering into my ear. After that we managed a sort of communication mainly by my following him and obeying his commanding glances and gestures and by his continuous use of "Te quiero Pedro." His deep voice and meaningful look whenever he said that made my stomach tense with a shiver that ran up through my body giving me a sensation veering between flying and the feeling you get when you make your first plunge into the sea on a cold day. We spent every day together but we never made love, Manolo treated me as if I were a virgin, paying court to me and making me feel very special. Mostly we danced or sat in bars holding hands and just feeling nice. Too soon the holiday was over, it was a sad last evening we spent in the Bar Derby holding hands and repeating Te quiero over and over. Manolo took Jim and I to the airport in a taxi, while Jim checked in with the tour guide and saw to the luggage, Manolo and I said our goodbyes with more Te quieros and hand holding, he wouldn't let me kiss him but the tears ran unashamedly down his face. When he finally left, too overcome with emotion to stay longer, I handed my ticket to the Stewardess, an English girl who said, "Is that your friend?" "Yes it is, can't you tell?" "He does look nice, never mind you can come back again, that's what happened to me, I came here on holiday, fell in love and when I went home I just got on the next plane back and I've been here ever since." I said that I didn't know if I felt that much about him. "You wait" she said, "You will, I'll bet you'll be back before you know it, the men are so different here, not like that lot back home." I thought that once back in England I would forget Manolo but when I reached home Vincent could tell somehow that something had happened. Without asking me and without any discussion, as soon as I got home and with my luggage still in the hall he pushed me into the bedroom and punched and beat me, hitting me with a piece of wood until I saw stars and my head was split open and bleeding. He relented enough and stopped so that I could get a taxi to St. James' Hospital, but he didn't come with me, I had to go alone. When I got to the hospital I had to wait for hours with the blood running down my neck because they had a big road crash to deal with. When it was finally my turn to be seen I had eight stitches in my head and four across the top of my eye. Even though the Doctor said it had been a serious injury it was treated as 'just a domestic' and I was left to find my own way home. I hadn't thought of returning to Las Palmas but Vincent's behaviour made it impossible for me to forget how nice it had been without all those rows and worries, the nice way I had felt when out with Manolo. Vincent didn't take me out at all, even when he was being nice to me. The more Vincent carried on the more I wished to be back and when I confided to a friend at work he said, "You are a fool Peter to put up with his jealousies, after all he doesn't stint himself and you do pay all the bills for the house, he should be more caring of you." Thinking back, maybe he wasn't just jealous of me but also jealous of the fact that my hard work could keep him in a nice way without too much effort on his part. My friend Shem spoke some Spanish and taught me the rudiments of the language while we sat working together. With his help I could soon telephone Manolo and say a few words to him while he played romantic records by Nino Bravo for me. In Gough Square near to the office was an adult education centre and each week there was a Spanish class from 12 to 1pm. I enrolled and could soon speak Spanish quite well. I telephoned Manolo every day. At the office wherever there was a telephone I picked it up and dialled all the digits, waiting for the tones that told me my call was winging its way across the ocean to Manolo. At first my calls were private but the more Spanish I learnt and the longer my conversations it was obvious to my colleagues what was happening. Every time I picked up a telephone I would hear, "Oh my God, he's at it again, phoning that man of his in Spain." Manolo was thrilled that I wanted to back again to see him and all my working hours were spent planning for the day when I could get back to see him. I managed to arrange my leave and in May I was back in Las Palmas. This time Manolo had enlisted the help of his brother-in-law who had rented a private apartment for me so that Manolo could stay with me. The first night we spent together we were both so shy, it was like the first time for both of us. Manolo was innocent in the ways of making love, just being naked and holding each other made his body shiver and shake and he came, wetting my belly each time. After three of those spontaneous ejaculations the next time I felt the hardness of his erection in my hand I guided him into me and he penetrated me with a shout and a scream as his body bucked and he rode me rising up each time as if he was a rodeo man determined to be the master. From then on it was like a wave engulfing us as Manolo experienced the joy that unfettered sex can bring, using me, touching me and kissing me in every secret place until I knew that this was where I should stay forever. Every mid-day we went to Manolo's house where his mother fed us, her daughters and grand-daughters spoiled me and fussed over me like I was part of the family. They were so pleased to see Manolo looking so happy and he, his eyes shining told me constantly how much he loved me "Pedro tu tenes venido para mi como un anjo del cielo jo voi sempre te quiero." Peter you came to me like an angel from the sky and I will always love you. These idyllic days soon passed and it was nearly time for me to return to England, I hated the thought of it and was determined that I would leave England and Vincent and return to Manolo in Las Palmas. I could sew, work in a bar, do anything I thought; Manolo's sister and her husband had just bought a new apartment on the edge of Las Palmas, the development overlooked the sea and the four apartment buildings were circular and looked like four lighthouses. I dreamed of buying an apartment somewhere like that, life would be so wonderful I thought. But life plays little tricks on us and leads us down many false passages. I came back to

England and started to save, when I told Manolo of my idea he asked me why he couldn't come to London. I thought well why not, he could work here easier than I could work there and we could eventually return together. Vincent and I were in a state of truce but not sleeping in the same room, he had intercepted some of Manolo's letters to me and knew exactly what had happened, another friend had translated them for him. When I had saved enough for the deposit on a house I looked for and found a nice house in Tooting, at that time it was £12,000. I began to prepare myself for the upheaval of leaving Streatham. Vincent begged me not to leave, crying for most of the day. I worried that he might not be able to pay the mortgage on his own, it never occurred to me that we should sell, I didn't want to make him leave his home. Then doubts crept into my mind, everyday when I telephoned Manolo, now that I could understand everything he said, I was subjected to a third degree of questioning, what, how, why was I doing. I remembered just how suspicious he had been when I talked to his brother (even though his brother was a fat idiot who didn't attract me at all) and once in a bar when a Briton talking to me refused to believe I wasn't Spanish. In the middle of my explanations as to why I wasn't speaking any English Manolo fell to the floor crying our "Mi corazon! Mi corazon!" The bar staff rushed to give him first aid but Manolo said, "Peter you are breaking my heart." Shades of Vincent I thought, I was landing myself with another jealous man. Determined to look my best for Manolo I had reduced my diet until I was barely ten stones and losing weight rapidly. In the December I developed a rash and my G.P. sent me to St. Georges hospital for a check up. When the nurse asked me to get on the scales I realised just how thin I was getting and then waiting to see the Doctor I noticed that this was the C Department. Immediately, wrongly, I thought that must mean cancer and what was happening now. Forgetting that my slimness was my own fault I panicked, 'Here am I probably about to find out something horrible and I still have so many things that I wish to do. All I do is live with one jealous man and then want to change him for another just as bad.' instantly I decided that if I didn't have cancer I would stop what I was doing and try to make a new start in my life. Of course I had panicked without reason, it was a simple matter, just needing a course of treatment with antibiotics and the 'C' on the Doctor's door had no significance. I left St. Georges on a cloud and went straight up to BOAC in Victoria and made a booking for Georgetown in Guyana for the next May. Also that day I abandoned my diet and ate about ten Mars bars.

I abandoned the house purchase and gradually stopped calling Manolo. Now writing this of course I regret it, remembering the niceness of the romance and walking hand in hand along the streets of Las Palmas. But at the time I was confused and much as I tried to resist Vincent exerted great pressure on me. He promised that things would change and be better, I would have no regrets and we would be happy like two turtledoves as he trotted out all the clichéd phrases to convince me he meant to be different. It wasn't much different really but it was different in that I went on my own to Amsterdam on December 31st to spend the New Year. The Amsterdam bars were full; after I checked in at a hotel I went straight out and joined them. As soon as I ordered my first drink it was paid for by a dashing man who insisted on taking me out to the other bars and then back to his apartment. We spent some hours on the pavement outside where everyone was setting off fireworks, the noise was deafening as the whole street made bang after bang, each bang meaning good luck for the new year so the more bangs the more good luck. As the dawn came the streets emptied and we went back into the apartment to drink brandy and eventually into his bed where he changed from the kind of man who opens doors and is very masculine to someone who said, "Fuck me fuck me I'm a woman." This wasn't for me at all so I told him I had a headache and that he should just go to sleep. As soon as possible in the morning I left and returned to the hotel where I ate a hearty Dutch breakfast, bathed and went to bed and slept. When I woke up it was about 2 o'clock and I went straight to the Thermos Sauna, I had been hearing about the Thermos for years. My good friend Shem painted a glowing picture about the delights of the place, the sex, the relaxation, the excitement, and here it was. There were so many different floors and so many people that it reminded me a lot of Electra House where I worked, except that Electra House was peopled by women as well as men and the product was telegrams. Here in the Amsterdam Thermos, there were only men and the product was sex. All the stories I had been hearing over the years were true, from the outside it just looked like two large houses facing the canal from which a faint haze of fog rose up. Then through the entrance door into a small foyer where you paid your entrance fee and received a locker key attached to an elastic wristband

and were told quite explicitly that this place was only for adult males of a certain persuasion. Collecting a bath towel I passed through into the locker room, from then on the atmosphere changed and the air was charged with the aroma of sex, the quiet sound of voices, some giggling, but not much, the touch of bare feet on the wooden floors as these liberated males prowled and paraded up and down and around the stairs that connected the two buildings. On the ground floor there was a full-length swimming pool set to one side and on the other side a bar where as it was New Years day everything was free, beers, wine and food. Up the staircase to the floors which had been turned into galleries lined with cubicles; these cubicles had a token, but not actually, of privacy through a scant curtain which could be pulled across, shading the cubicle but giving visual access to any passer-by who cared to look and outside one or two – where inside a particularly energetic coupling was taking place – a group of men jostled each other in order to see everything. This close proximity led to more arousal and couples broke away to find a cubicle of their own. I walked around and up and down hardly believing what I could see, I had several drinks at the free bar and when a red haired man made it clear that he liked me I went with him to search for a cubicle of our own, he didn't really want anyone else to watch him but it was unavoidable so I pulled him down to me and whispered gently in his ear that he should pretend we were alone, he was soon aroused and satisfied, then he hurried away covered as much in his confusion as by his towel to shower and regain his anonymity. He had been satisfied quickly but I had merely been aroused by the encounter, my years with

Vincent had accustomed me to participate in the sexual act for hours rather than minutes. I walked around and then back to the bar but I didn't see anybody that looked capable enough for me. On my way round the building I had seen some men disappearing into a darkened part of the top floor and after more alcohol found the courage to investigate. The darkened passage opened out into another room, quite large with couches along one wall. At first this was all I could see and I though that this must be where they came to sleep. The only illumination in this room was from a small bulb high in the ceiling with a fluorescent quality, that glowed slightly blue, which made the wrist-band glow and I noticed that I looked tanned. Suddenly my eyes adjusted completely to the light and I could see that the room was full of men, as many in that one room as there were in the whole of the rest of the building. Without exception every male was engaged in sexual activity, kissing, touching, performing oral sex on one while he was being kissed and fondled by another, hands, fingers and penis were being used to penetrate the ever-willing receivers of the attentions of the more aggressive males. For me, who had spent so much of my life in an enclosed relationship this was revelation and I was losing control. The alcohol, the smell of amytal in the air and the pure male odour made me reel with the excitement and moving to the centre of a dense crowd of men I abandoned myself to hours of pleasure, my body was used in every way possible, I kissed and satisfied so many men that I had no way of knowing exactly how many it was. At last I began to tire and in those pre-condom days between my legs down to my knees were wet and I needed to shower. I thought it was time that I had another drink and saw that I had been in that dark room for four hours. I was enjoying myself with my drink and laughing with a Dutchman over the antics of some Germans who were trying to get as much of the free celebratory food as possible. I looked towards the swimming pool and coming towards me was a tall dark man with long curly hair falling wet around his face. When he got close to me and said hello I knew by his accent that he was from Spain, at once I remembered Manolo and felt warm and close to this man. He took a drink from the bar and stood close to me his body wetting me through my clean towel. We drank together and stood enjoying each other's company. "I know we have only just met but would you come to a cubicle with me? he asked. Pushing away the thoughts of what had happened during the last four hours I said yes I would like to as I hadn't been upstairs yet, I wanted to respond to his gentle approach. We found a cubicle and he made love to me gently and considerately with a natural firmness that I appreciated. When we left the cubicle we went straight to the showers where we washed each other and then when we had dressed we left together and went to a bar that was full of people from Surinam. It was New Year, the landlord fed all of us on the house and every fifteen minutes or so a bell rang and that meant that the drinks were free as well. This man Xavier, told me that he was a doctor in Madrid – a paediatrician – he had recently lost his boyfriend and had been very unhappy until he met me this afternoon, "Please come out with me tonight Peter," he asked me, hiss English was excellent, at least I didn't have to struggle with my Spanish in order to communicate. We agreed that we would go to a club and dance all night. Xavier escorted me to my hotel, the owner was very impressed with him, but it seemed odd to me that in this city with all its temptations they placed a lot of emphasis on romance. By the time Xavier called for me I had washed my hair and changed, I felt really good, the release of the afternoon's pleasure and meeting him had made me feel vibrant and very alive. We were at the club having a romantic evening holding hands and dancing close together when I suddenly though ' what is happening her, I am doing it again, everyone else comes to Amsterdam to make love with lots of strangers and here am I behaving like a first time lover' and then when a man asked me to dance Xavier sent him away, his face clouded with possessiveness and jealousy; I decided that it was time for me to wake up, after all what could come of this affair, nothing but another enclosure of love and I already had Vincent to contend with at home. I told Xavier that I needed to go to the toilet and wouldn't be long but he was sulking and didn't answer me, that confirmed my action and I left the club and him. It was late when I got back to the hotel and as I was the last guest to arrive back they locked the doors behind me, I was pleased about this as I had a thought that Xavier might follow me and cause a scene. The next morning I flew back to London and that episode of my life closed leaving me with memories to relive later on.

When I got back to London Vincent was busy with a new guest at the house, one of his teacher friends had recommended a lady from India to us. This lady ran a boarding school in Northern India and as most of her pupil's parents were wealthy and paid her fees into account outside India she had a lot of money in England

and the United States of America. Mrs Buck dressed only in pure silk saris the whole time and confided to me how sorry she was that we had to live in England and that at least in India we can still have servants. I thought yes and given my circumstances if I lived there I would probably be one of those servants. Mrs. Buck suites Vincent to a T., they got on very well and having her there to interest him with her tales of wealth and luxury kept him from too much third degree about what I had done in Amsterdam. I started back to work the next day and recommenced doing as much overtime as possible so that I could take enough money with me when I went to Guyana in May. May in Guyana is the rainy season but in their rain you don't get cold just temporarily wet and then the sun shines, the skies clear and everyone is dry and hot again. Before I left London I had written to Vincent's uncle and arranged to stay with him. In his welcoming letter he gave me a list of items apparently unobtainable in Guyana, which he said he would like me to take with me. Mrs. Butters, Moma, wrote in reply to my letter that if I did want to bring anything she would be glad but no she didn't need anything except to see me at last. No one accompanied me to the airport, Vincent didn't really want me to go and tried to ignore that I was going. I took a taxi to Victoria and then the airways bus to Heathrow where we boarded the plane, it looked so small to be travelling so far but I had my Valium and once on the plane a large brandy, the combination took care of any minor quibbles I had about the flight and by moving me seat to join a jolly chatty handsome man with a bottle of rum the rest of the journey was plain sailing. Ovid and I laughed and talked our way across the Atlantic. The plane made several stops in the West Indies and although the islands looked pretty from the air the airports were dry and dusty. Then suddenly, half an hour out of Barbados I looked down and saw this vast land covered with lush green trees and huge rivers and there we were at last flying over the South American Continent. Situated on the edge of the Atlantic sea, Guyana is also on the edge of the Amazon Basin and shares the rich vegetation that tropical heat combined with bountiful water makes possible.

CHAPTER ELEVEN.

As soon as I stood on Guyanese land I knew, in spite of the intense heat that I had reached home, I felt comfortable as if I had always been there. But my first thoughts were for the people who had been brought here years ago; after a horrific journey from Africa in a crowded ship being expected to work hard in the sugar fields. The customs men at Timheri airport, notorious in London, treated me with a friendship and welcome that confirmed to me that I was at home. The feeling I had was the same as I had when my mother had taken me to her home in Yorkshire for the first time, I belonged to both places equally. I had started to realise why my mother had compared Vincent to my father that first day when I took him to meet her.

Ovid and I came out of the customs post together; crowds of people were at the barrier to meet friends and relatives. Walter had sent one of his nephews to meet me and it was easy for him to recognise me as I was the only white person coming from the airplane. We took a taxi to

Walters house, the journey passed in a sort of haze, I was very tired and still under the influence of too much rum. Walter's house was a large three storey building in a wide tree lined avenue with a promenade in the middle like the boulevards in France or North Africa. When I walked through Walter's front door and up the stairs which entered straight into his sitting room, it took my breath away, it was clear that this where Vincent grew up and this is where he learnt to hoard everything in sight. This sitting room of Uncle Walter's was crammed from end to end with furniture, life-size models of tigers and bears, carvings, cabinets filled with china and glass, pictures covered the walls and stuffed animals and large toys used any vacant space. This sitting room was even bigger than our room had been in Wandsworth Common where we had held those big parties. No wonder Vincent liked to have our house filled and crowded with things. The only real living space in this enormous house was a small space at the top of the stairs where there was a long bench and three chairs, all wooden and hard, the comfortable furniture was covered up with the ornaments and bric a brac. Uncle Walter greeted me and the nephew that had accompanied me from the airport left for the evening. Uncle Walter and I sat on the hard chairs while he told me how hard it was to live in Guyana and how lucky we were to be able to live 'outside' in England or like his other nephew in New York.

Uncle Walter's idea of a hard life was to have his cupboards crammed full with tins, jars and packets of food, his bedroom had an en-suite shower that he couldn't use because of the four sacks of rice stored there. He had asked me, amongst other thing, to bring from London a bath towel and some cologne, I gave these to him and put them away. The towel cupboard reached from the ceiling to the floor and was full of every colour towel you can imagine, it was like a mini Department Store and the other wall was lined with a cupboard which was filled with toiletries of all descriptions, soap, colognes, creams, oils, ointments, hairbrushes, combs and enough bath oils to keep an Avon lady busy for months. Uncle Walter's house stood on a large plot of land on which there were three other houses, a two storey house at the back which was surrounded by avocado and carambola trees which were so abundant with fruit that the ones that fell to the ground were just left there, it was so easy to pick a just ripe avocado or carambola from the tree when you wanted to. In the other corner was a three-storied house occupied by three families and in the centre a low building with three bedrooms for Walter's older sisters. Situated below sea level Guyana is protected by a strong sea wall with most of the houses built up on stilts. Small trenches run along the roads with small bridges connecting the houses to the road; these trenches gradually get larger as they run out towards the sea. There is a small village called Plaisance which is near to the sea wall, the air is fresher than it is in Georgetown and the trenches on each side of the road are something like 12 feet wide, these trenches filled with pink water lilies and with the trees on each side of the road bending towards each other forming a brilliant green arch make you feel that you are in the middle of an exotic film set. I stayed in Guyana for six weeks and at first I thought that I was going to find difficulty in exploring the country at all. Walter thought that I shouldn't go out alone for fear of the dreaded 'choke and rob', which is Guyana's version of mugging. I tried to tell him that we had muggings in England and indeed in all parts of the world but he continued to worry about me. One day I went to visit Moma alone and she begged me not to do it again especially as I was wearing my two gold rings. "They can tell that you are a stranger and those rings, please take them off at once." To please her I took off the rings and stuffed them into my pocket and hid them in Walter's house when I got back. Moma and her daughters had different ideas to Vincent and Walter; you could sit in their sitting rooms and walk about easily. "We all know what you mean by the confusion at Uncle Walter," said Hyacinth, Vincent's youngest sister, and we know that Vincent grew up like that as well." The two men were so alike they could have been twins except that Walter was thirty years older than Vincent and his circle of young boys were referred to as 'nephews' and Vincent called his friends 'cousins'. At first Walter was very friendly towards me but after I failed to understand the significance of a visit by a close friend of his who disappeared into Walter's bedroom, Walter's attitude changed towards me and he began to treat me somewhat distantly, the same way he treated one of his blood nephews who wasn't interested in his schemes and who they all referred to as 'the black one', light skin being still desirable amongst the crowd that grew up in the midst of colonialism. This black one, Linden, was the one I got on with the best. If I asked him to buy a bottle of rum for me he would bring back the exact change, whereas the fair skinned 'nephew' who came to the airport would never have change, Linden took great pleasure in showing me his Georgetown and introduced me to his girlfriend to whom he gave any dollars I handed him as a reward for shopping for me. Aunt Patience who I had first met in London was back in Georgetown where she practised physiotherapy. Known always as Nurse Forrester the Guyana Health Minister visited her and confirmed her qualifications were such that she could assume the title of Doctor Forrester. Aunt Patience came to Walter's and escorted me out to visit the big market. Dominated by an enormous clock at its entrance, Stabroek Market was a cornucopia of vegetables and fruit. Piles of water coconuts, sapodillas, mangoes, paw paws, bunches of long Bora beans, bananas of many shapes, sizes, colours and names and leafy green vegetables in profusion. I had my first ever taste of jelly coconut, the vendor, a dark handsome beauty flashed her teeth at me in pleasure at my enjoyment of the soft white coconut jelly that I scooped out with the scoop that she had fashioned from the first cut of the green fruit. I had tasted sapodillas before but not like this, the hard grainy fruit that I had sampled in England faded into unreality compared with the luscious heady scented fruits that I ate walking round the market with Patience. These trips with Linden and Patience were enjoyable but I did want to see the other side of Georgetown and I didn't like my day finishing at 5 o'clock, which is when they thought a tourist should be safely inside the house. Then one morning, Michael – one of Guyana's blue eyed tanned men – who lived in the house at the end of the garden, came to take me to visit a school master friend of Walter's. I think the original plan was that I was to be especially friendly but Michael stayed for a long time and the schoolmaster wasn't able to make his wishes known to me. We sat on the open balcony overlooking the street and Michael and I were on our second bottle of rum when a young man called hello from the street, they invited him up and introduced him to me. Orin was a pretty mixture boy with Chinese and Black ancestry who would have been very suited to Vincent had he been there. Orin and I got on well and he asked the others, "Why don't we take Peter out, he can't just sit around all the time, he is on holiday after all." They decided to take me to a club restaurant called 'Rendezvous' I knew that Ruth had worked there years ago and I looked forward to seeing it. Rendezvous was a double first for me, this was when I realised the Guyana's predilection for ice in large quantities; accompanying four beers was enough ice to satisfy a London pub for a whole night and it was the first time that both men and women queued to dance with me. By the time we reached the Rendezvous I had consumed a lot of alcohol and after two beers any inhibitions vanished. "Orin" I said, "I do like the tune they are playing now, I wish I could dance." "Get up and dance if you want to, everyone does," said Orin. As I left my seat and went towards the small dance floor I heard "What's that white man doing?" but I didn't care and once on the dance floor something took over me and I danced with abandon, suddenly I was the centre of attraction – the men jostled each other to gain a position in front of me as I danced and wined down to the floor and up again. "Uh, Uh, how you a white man an you can wine up like dat – you like a real niga bwoy" a strong man called to me as I wined but instantly he was pushed aside by a young woman who said "Now it's my turn to dance with him, we all waitin" and there was a stream of men and women claiming their turn to dance with me.

When a break in the music let me return to the table it was covered with drinks sent for me, glasses and bottles of rum, more than even I could drink. From then on everywhere I went I was recognised. Later that night Orin told the others that he would see me home but instead of going home we went on to the 'Belvedere' which is a night club in the grounds of one of the large colonial houses in Main Street. The garden had walls of bamboo, so although enclosed it was open to the sky, illuminated mostly by the coloured lights from underneath the dance floor where I went straight away to dance until the morning. There the men allowed me to dance alone but stood on the edge of the floor calling softly and loudly their appreciation of my movements and my white skin. Their remarks didn't endear me to the Indian girls standing along the sides waiting to be noticed and the next night when I went back with Orin the doorman tried to keep me out. "They sayin you bad and not to come in" he said, but a Chinese girl came to the gate and told him that it was only the Indian girls that were jealous of me but she knew that I was not in competition with them and that he should let me enter. "But he is dancing with men in there." I said, "Well why not? all the men in Guyana dance together, what's wrong with that?" The only difference is that I have this" pointing to my hand I played a trump card, "Just because I'm different is no reason not to let me in, I can't help being white." This threw him into confusion as I played the prejudice card my own way and he flung open the gates and I was a welcome guest every time I went after that. Most days I slept until 9 o'clock, after breakfast I sat next to the front window with Walter who received many visitors, like

Vincent he was a focal point for many different people – politicians, actors, business men and many relatives all coming to him for advice or help. Orin came in the afternoons and Walter thought it safe for me to go onto the streets with him. Orin and I went across the whole of Georgetown, Camp Street, Water Street, Main Street and into Guyana Stores which were still known as Bookers and Fogertys – the two department stores taken into public ownership but still using the stationery with the names from the colonial days. Outside the stores I bought lottery tickets but didn't win. A turn into the Tower Hotel where sharp sexy Asian boys served ice cold beers while the locals 'limed' just hanging around, watching the few tourists and salesmen from the islands using the swimming pool. Orin knew everyone and everywhere to go, he carried a parcel under his arm which I suspected was Marijuana going by his secret confidences with men in doorways, it can't all have been about me although he had many enquiries about the availability of his white friend. After leaving Belvedere late one night we were walking along Water Street at about 1 o'clock when we were surrounded by men, unshaven men wearing high necked sweaters, "Quickly get in" they said ushering us towards a closed transit van parked alongside 'so this is the choke and rob' I thought, but as soon as we got inside the van I saw the dogs and heard a voice "Come in Peter, have a drink." These were policemen on night patrol, they knew Orin and had heard about me; we stayed talking and drinking for the rest of the night reaching home about six in the morning. Wherever I went in Georgetown I met policemen, they bought me beers, ice creams and milkshakes, making me feel at home and welcome. After that experience I had no difficulty in understanding the problems Caribbeans find with English policemen.

Orin came early one morning to take me to Linden which is 67 miles from Georgetown on the Demerara River. We went by bus on the new highway, a long straight road lined with farms and pineapple plantations, Guyana pineapples are as big as watermelons and very sweet. After a few miles most of us fell asleep only waking up when the bus made a sharp turn into the outskirts of Linden. I hadn't realised that Linden was a new name given to the area that included the famous mining town of Mackenzie and the villages across the Demerara of Wismar and Christiansburg. I did know that Vincent's oldest sister Valda lived in Wismar. We stopped by the riverbank to buy a drink and listen to the music (and be chatted to by young miners wearing their hard hats and proffering Cashews which are like bright red apples with a white flesh and all promising wild delights if I would meet them for a drink later on). Looking across the river I could see the sawmill belonging to Hyacinths father-in-law. "Look Orin, I know those people, they'll tell me where Valda lives, I wouldn't like to come this far and not see her." Orin said, "We have to cross the river but I don't know where the ferry is and the bridge is a long way from here." One of the miners directed us to the ferry which was more like a canoe with an outboard motor, when the passengers were onboard the top of the side was level with the river. I had no qualms on the way across but as soon as we got out I couldn't believe that I had made the crossing in that small unsafe looking craft. However we were over, there would be time enough to think about the return later on. Mr. King had heard of me and was pleased to entertain us and later had his driver take us further inland to meet Valda. Vincent had sent her pictures of me and she rushed out of her house to meet me coming up the drive, hugging me welcome as if she knew me already, because of Moma they all treated me like another brother. After we all had drank fresh mango juice and eaten slices of the obligatory Creole pound cake Mr. King's driver took us back to the sawmill. The sawmill built on the edge of the river and parts of it overhang the water. Guyana hospitality continued at the sawmill and after a few bottles of Banks beer I needed to use the toilet that was in the part of the building overhanging the river. The toilet itself looked ordinary enough but when I lifted the seat cover I saw that everything went straight down into the river where a cluster of fish waited. This was similar to the one at the ferry station except that there the detritus was dealt with by a host of small insects. Later that night after we had all visited the Chinese store to eat fried rice and chow mein, Mr. King drove us back to Georgetown crossing by the bridge so I didn't have to worry about the small ferry. When Mr. King dropped us off near to the bus terminal waiting for us was one of the mechanics who had been servicing the bus that morning. We smiled and he came across "I have been waiting for you to come back," he said with a slow smile, "I would like to have an English friend like you." He wasn't a handsome man but young, tall and heavily built with a head like a bull, full faced and fleshy, his eyelids lowered as he stared full into my fact. I gave him my address in London and he promised to write to me. When I got home I did receive a letter from him 'When are you coming back to Guyana?' he wrote, 'When I saw you that morning and you smiled my cock got hard and I dreamt you all night.' Later that week Orin and I had an argument with a guard outside Demicos' ice cream parlour and had to go to the main police station next door to the big market. The Sergeant in charge talked to Orin and then came over to me. I thought he would ask me questions about what had happened. His six foot muscular frame leant over me and he told me that he wanted an English friend, just like the mechanic except that he didn't want to write, he wanted an English friend right here and now. I had to go with him to an interview room at the back of the station where he 'interrogated' me several times, making me lie, stand and sit until we were both exhausted with the heat and the pleasure.

Orin was waiting outside for me, "From the noise coming out of that room I thought you were being beaten or something" he said, "But here you are looking rosy and pleased with yourself, what happened in there?" I said, "It's a police matter and I can' discuss it." Orin laughed, "I saw how he looked at you, you don't need to tell me anything, the whole station knew what was happening in there."

All things considered I thought the Georgetown Policemen wonderful.

Adventure was the key word while Orin was around. We went by ferry to Vreed-En-Hoop, which is on the west bank of the Demerara River. When we alighted there was a fleet of taxi cars waiting to take passengers on to Parika on the Essequibo River and with about eight others we got ourselves squashed into the one with the nicest looking driver. Orin and I got out of the taxi just before Parika so that he could show me the overgrown remains of one of the discarded railway tracks. Guyanese consider with pride the former railway system and mourn its loss that came about as part of the sweeping away of colonial ideas. At a bend in the road there was a small guesthouse with a bar, we went in for a drink. The Purple Heart stood alone on a huge plot with goats and chickens and other livestock wandering around giving it a real country air; above the bar were seven guest rooms with showers. Morning turned to afternoon and we graduated from a bottle of Banks beer drank by ourselves to bottles of rum drank at a large table with the owner and his friends. We were joined by the taxi car driver who had been looking for us and guessed where we would be. Making no secret of his liking for me he bought another bottle of rum for the party and a bottle of vodka for me. The other men joked with him, "Is why yuh buy de vodka, yuh tink yuh get a chance wit dat ting?" He didn't answer them, but held me with his eyes as if we were there alone. He was a tall 'Dougla' man, that mixture of Black and Asian that showed in his loose black curls and refined flaring nostrils and full, yet not too full mouth. When he moved closer to me and said, "Me is suh black and yuh is so white, come, yuh go up de stairs and mek me get a room for us." I was lost. Intoxicated as much by his attentions as by the rum and vodka, I went up the stairs without hesitation. He joined me in the upper corridor and guided me into the room, using his big hands to control my movement.

I hadn't sunbathed so my skin was still very pale, contrasting with his muscled blue/black body when he undressed and threw himself upon me. His hands held firmly onto my ankles lifting my legs so high that I thought they must surely snap off. He was erect and veiny like a stallion, entering me with such a force that for the first time in my life I bled like a virgin. He thrust inside my body, pulling our completely each time and re-entering with a pressure that I felt along the whole of my spine. Then when it seemed as if I couldn't take more, he stopped and kissed me and held me very tightly telling me how much he enjoyed me. Although I had been at the point of begging him to stop, as soon as he did stop I wanted him back inside me. We bathed and went downstairs to join the others who gave knowing looks. "You were right overhead," said Orin "and I thought you would come through the ceiling any minute." "But we were only talking" I said, without convincing anyone.

Needing to get some air and be alone for a moment to collect my thoughts I went outside, it had grown dark and here, outside the town there were no street lights and no houses for miles, the night enclosed the trees and all traces of the road. It was impossible to see anything until I looked upwards and boy nothing had prepared me for the sight of the sky under those conditions. The clean clear air and the blackness made the sky seem close to the earth, I didn't know it was possible to see so many stars at once, glistening and moving across the heavens, the stars were so bright I felt as if I could launch myself into space with ease. I felt someone close quickly behind me, it was my 'Dougla Man' "Come Petes, let's go back to the bed, I need to finish off." "I thought you had finished?" "No Petes, I was enjoying it so much I wanted it to last but I am wanting to cum now." He closed in on me and I could smell his body, eager and sexual, hot and masculine. Helplessly in the middle of a living fantasy I return with him to the room upstairs where after another hour of coupling he screamed obscenities at me and jerked his body so hard I felt pain up to the top of my head. "This is a man chile yuh getting" he shouted, as his body bucked and rode me to the finish. After this he left me in the room alone and later on Orin came upstairs and said that we should stay here until morning as it was now too late to go back to Georgetown. "Where has that man got to?" I asked Orin, "Is he staying as well?"

"No Peter, he has gone home, to his wife I should think." We both slept well that night and early in the morning we showered and went downstairs. In the bar were the remains of the drinking session, glasses, bottles and filled ashtrays. Orin busied himself in cleaning up the place. "I'll do this Peter, you sit down and I'll get you some coffee in a moment, if I clean up for the man he won't want to charge us for staying here." When he had finished cleaning and I was drinking my coffee, Orin chatted to the man who was pleased to see his bar so nice and clean that early in the morning. "Don't go yet, he said, the taxi car man is coming back to take you to Vreed-En-Hoop so that you can get the ferry back across to Georgetown." 'Dougla Man' came back later and looked even better in the daylight. I heard him tell the bar owner that "The wife give me hell man!" He drove us back to the ferry in silence but asked Orin if he would bring me back the next weekend, even after what had happened the day before he seemed unsure how to talk to me that morning. I agreed that we would go back and he waved us on to the ferry. Back at the house Walter was furious with me for staying out all night

"Orin you should know I would worry, what would I tell my nephew if Peter came to any harm while he is in my house?" I was in no mood to argue or explain and went to my room leaving Orin to do the explaining and pacifying, he was very good at that. The rest of that week Orin and I drifted about Georgetown as usual. He called for me around 3pm and we toured the shops and streets until late each night usually finished up at the Belvedere where we knew we would be well treated and not have to pay for anything. I wanted to go to see the famous Kaiteur Falls which had the highest single drop waterfall in the world being 226m – five times the height of the much visited Niagara falls. Unfortunately only one plane a week was flying out to Kaiteur and it was fully booked for the whole time that I was there, everyday it was one of our stops to check for any cancellations but we were disappointed each time. On Saturday we prepared to go back to Parika, when we reached Vreed-En-Hoop my 'Dougla Man' wasn't there but he had sent a friend to take us to The Purple Heart guesthouse with a message that we were to wait for him there. Orin and I settled down at a table with a bottle of rum and a platter filled with small pieces of fried chicken surrounding a red well of tomato ketchup mixed with hot pepper sauce. I began to feel an excitement at the thought of the night to come. Suddenly at the door was an outraged black woman, tall and strong, wielding a machete in one hand and a voice that sent a chill. "Where dat bitch? She wan tek me man she gon tek mi too, me gon give her a chop wi dis she gon member long time." The owner of the Purple Heart spoke to her and from the ensuing garbled conversation Orin and I realised that she was 'Dougla Man's wife and she had found out he was meeting someone and assumed it was a woman, luckily for me she had not thought he might be meeting a man. Wasting no time, Orin took up the small bag that I had used to carry my razor and toothbrush in. Calling out to the owner of the bar as we sped away that we had people waiting and had to catch the ferry. "Oh my God" I said, "Orin what an escape, if he had met us and been there what would I have done?" "Don't think about if, forget that now, we won't go back there – someone might tell her about you – she is shouting too much." Rather than go straight back to Georgetown we went from the guesthouse in to Parika. In the small street market I bought small pink bananas and small sweet nutty fruits called cockrits, we drank coconut water and a little rum. Parika is on the Essequibo River and as we were there I knew I just had to go somewhere on that river. We decided to go to Leguan Island which is about 18 square miles large and where they grow a lot of rice. The Essequibo River is very wide, it was like crossing the English Channel, we were soon out of sight of land and it took more than an hour to reach the island. The ferry tied up at the Stellin or Quay. (Many of Guyana's words carry the touch of the Dutch that once ruled the country.) The long jetty led to a sandy shore ringed around with houses. As the ferry wouldn't return until the next day we tried to find a room for the night, unfortunately as it was the weekend the two guesthouses were full. We made our way to the Police Station where the constable in charge said we would be welcome to stay. I asked him the best place to go for something to eat and drink. "I'll show you myself, just let me close the station." He locked the door and the three of us went across the road to a bar. Orin and I ate and then bought a bottle of rum, the afternoon turned into evening, the constable and I danced – a crowd of boys soon joined us, all competing to catch my attention by dancing with abandon. By the time we decided to go back to the station it was dark and the constable had disappeared. Orin and I approached the station and the angry Sergeant in charge, furious at finding the station unmanned when he came on duty, refused to let us set foot in the place – threatening to shoot us if we didn't go away. Orin and I walked along the main street not sure what to do. One of the boys that had been in the bar suggested we should ask the guard on the Stellin if we could sleep there, but I didn't fancy wandering out along that long jetty, there was no light and not much moon shining. A group of three young men stopped and asked Orin what was happening. When he explained the situation they said that we should go with them. We followed the three boys down a dark road, the moon started to shine but it was still difficult to see and I couldn't make out any houses along the road. I began to wonder what I was getting into now when they stopped and we were in front of a weatherboard house. It was very late but they woke up their mother and sisters who welcomed us and insisted on feeding us before they emptied one of their bedrooms, giving us fresh linen and wishing us goodnight.

So it was the five of us in one room.

Orin lay down on the single bed leaving the big double bed for me and the three boys who made no secret of what would happen next, it was just a case of them agreeing who would be the first. Orin pretended to be asleep, the two younger boys led me downstairs through a trapdoor to the bottom of the house, down there the scent of the trees and the river combined with the darkness forming and aphrodisiac that sent the two boys on a wild extravagance of sex, each trying to outdo the other using my mouth and body in turn until they could do no more. My part was the easier and when we went back up the staircase I was eager then to see what would happen with the boy still in bed. He was a slower more dedicated lover, taking time throughout the night using long deep thrusts that satisfied more than the frenzied hurry of the others. When we woke the next morning, the boys, now sober, searched the bedroom for any signs of sexual activity and begged me not to let anyone know what had happened. The eldest sister cooked breakfast for all of us, fried eggs, stewed beef, fried yellow plantain and fresh Creole bread. I had a good appetite and ate a lot. After I had exchanged addresses with the family we left to make out way back to the Stellin and the ferry. Orin said, "Boy, how do you do it? All that sex and rum and you can eat a breakfast like that and you look good too, it's wearing me out and I'm not doing anything like you are." I was lucky to have met Orin; he had appointed himself as my watchdog and no matter what inducements he stayed sober and refused all invitations to leave with any of the men that talked to us. Just like the Sri Lankans in Egypt he was a guardian angel for me. It was blowing on the river that morning and the water was choppy but I was full of contentment, staying up on the top deck to get the full effect of the breeze and watch the island of Leguan disappear as we headed for Parika. A party of Indian men were on board going to a wedding at a village called Middle Dam. The bridegroom sat near to me, resplendent in his wedding robes; clear pink trousers and robe, wearing a triple wedding crown of gold hung with coloured stones, around his neck he wore many gold chains and his fingers were covered with rings. He didn't talk to me but just sat smiling shyly, his father smiled at me and sat close to me telling me of the wedding to come that day and showing me the casket of jewels they were carrying for the bride. "You must come to the wedding," he said. I had heard about the Indian weddings in Guyana and knew that this was something not to be missed. When we disembarked at Parika the wedding party were whisked away by car, the wedding would last all day so there was no hurry for us to get there. I went back to the café for some coffee and then when we had exhausted all the possibilities of Parika, Orin and I set off down the long road leading to Middle Dam. On one side of the road was a deep trench – like a small river – dissected with a wooden bridge wherever there was a house and the women had started to do their washing, dipping the clothes into the trench and banging the cloth onto the boards of the small bridges. Once outside Georgetown the women could wear their jewellery without fear and the sound of banging cloth was accompanied by the jangling, tinkling sound of the many bracelets adorning the wrists and the golden chains around their ankles. We received several invitations to stop for tea and chat, while we stopped drinking tea and talking about Guyana and England the young boys of the families would disappear to climb the many mango trees and bring us back large ripe mangoes sticky and heavy with perfume which we ate, the juice dripping down our arms...Gradually the road filled with people as we got nearer to the wedding house, the smell of curry and the sound of music filled the air and there we were. The wedding was occupying two houses, underneath the first house was the wedding ceremony taking place watched over by the female relatives and friends of the couple who were seated underneath a bower of leaves and flowers, both shyly smiling, their robes covered with dollar bills pinned on to them by the guests. I pinned my offering on to the robe of the groom and one of the two priests conducting the ceremony smiled a blessing at me and touched me with the bunch of leaves that he held in his hand. After what I thought was a polite interval I made my way over to the second house where the men were gathered and were serving the food. The food was served into big leaves and we all ate with our fingers, what was left on the leaf plates was just thrown into a corner of the garden for the dogs to look at and whatever they left was quickly recycled by the insects. No pollution, no washing up or paper plates to dispose of, I thought it a marvellous idea and a pity I couldn't transfer it to London. As the men finished their food, the music was played louder and the rum bottles passed around more quickly. We all danced until some of the men fell down but I managed to stay upright until someone with a car took us down to where we could get a bus up to Vreed-En-Hoop and the ferry back to Georgetown. When we got back to Georgetown it was already dark but instead of going straight back to Hatfield Street we stopped at a Chinese restaurant so that I could have some soup. I had a fancy for some Won-Ton soup and consumed a large tureen full. Orin didn't like it but I loved the greenness of the vegetable and the taste of the dumplings.

It was very late when we got back to Walter's and again he was cross and upset with me; the grapevine had already told him that Peter had been dancing in a low life bar in Leguan and later disporting himself with abandon at an Indian wedding. I couldn't see that it was much to worry about, just the dancing, at least he hadn't known about the taxi car man's wife and my near miss at disaster. After so much drinking that day I was in an argumentative mood and certainly not in the mood to listen. After shouting at Walter for half an hour I packed my suitcase and prepared to leave. Walter began to panic, "How can you go out on your own in the night?"

"You should have thought of that before, I don't care, I'm going!" With that I stormed out of the house dragging my suitcase along the ground, but once outside I wondered at the wisdom of my action especially when encumbered by my luggage.

Once again the Georgetown Police sprang into action. Coming out of the house next door was a tall dark man with a bicycle. As he came towards me he smiled and said "Hello Peter, what are you doing?" I didn't recognise him and asked him how he knew my name. "I am a Police and I know all about you, where are you going?"

I told him that I wanted to go to the other end of Hatfield Street and needed help with my suitcase. He picked up my heavy suitcase with ease and rested it across the handlebar of his bicycle and we walked down the street to where Vincent's sister Hyacinth lived, although she didn't expect me at that time she showed no surprise at my appearing. She told me later that she had heard from Uncle Walter and had expected me to leave his house before now. Hyacinth said that Walter was too old for young people, she was more diplomatic than Aunt Patience who said, "It's just because Walter can't make a profit from you if you don't go with the men he chooses and that made him disagreeable with you." I only had another week in Guyana which went much too quickly but I did manage to visit the Botanical Gardens which include a small zoo with and elephant and a large lake filled with manatees that came to the side when you whistled. The high spot of the Botanical Gardens for me was to see the statue of Queen Victoria that had been removed from it's plinth in Main Street when Guyana became independent and which was now installed in the centre of a pond filled with those gigantic Victoria water lilies.

On the morning of my departure Hyacinth arranged for her driver to take me with Moma and cousin Iris to the airport. Although she rarely left her house Moma was a well-known and loved personality and greeted by all the staff at the airport who were pleased to see her. While we waited for the plane to be called we said our last goodbyes and I left Georgetown with tears streaming down my face.

On board the plane the stewardess sat me next to a very light skinned middle-aged couple who said that they were "So pleased to be going home at last, these people are so noisy." I had found Georgetown very quiet but I understood that what they really meant was to ally themselves with me as a white man. They asked me if I had been on business so I told them that I had been visiting my relatives who all lived in Guyana, this quietened them but I moved to another seat anyway and this time was lucky to sit next to a young man who was coming to London to visit his mother, he had always lived out of town in a small village called Glasgow and not even been to Georgetown before. When we arrived at Heathrow he was astounded at its size and thought that he was in London already. "Wait until you get to London" I told him, this is nothing compared to that.

His mother and her boyfriend came to meet him and as no one was meeting me I took a taxi home.

CHAPTER TWELVE.

Vincent had received a telephone call from Uncle Walter with a garbled, well anyway his, version of what had happened. According to Walter I had men sleeping in the garden all night waiting for me, they were practically queuing up is how he put it. Vincent and I had a big row and I collected another trophy in the form of a scar on my wrist from a blow he gave me with a hot pot-spoon. After that life went back to our version of normal, with me working every day and Vincent staying at home. I worked every day possible, especially on Public holidays that were double-time. We didn't seem to get any good permanent tenants in the house and for some reason the supply of Egyptians wanting to stay slowed down, although we still catered for the odd wedding and made cakes the house still needed a lot of money to keep going and I didn't want Vincent to lapse into his old profession; I had already found, hidden under the eaves in the loft a parcel containing a syringe and some penicillin which I took and threw away. When I asked Vincent why it was there he denied all knowledge of it but I felt sure it had been his. At work the main topic of conversation was 'Early Retirement' and 'Redundancy Payments' anybody over fifty years with a fairly long service could retire early and have a lump sum of money with a pension to follow. Many of the older colleagues were leaving to start businesses, guesthouses, corner shops, butchers and dress shops. I began to wish that I were in that position so that both Vincent and I could be occupied. At the back of my mind was always the fear that he would be tempted to re-commence abortions and I didn't want to go through that again. Overnight, or so it seemed the value of our house had jumped from £7,000 to £24,000 and looked like going even higher. I suggested to Vincent that we could sell the house and buy a shop with living accommodation above; that way he could run the shop and I could still work until we were busy enough for me to stop working or until I could get a good redundancy deal. He liked the idea and I began to look for something suitable. For most of 1978 I looked at shops. I went to Croydon, Stoke Newington, Stamford Hill, Peckham, Wimbledon and as far away as Hampton Court without success but then Vincent said that he had seen a shop in Clapham High Street that might be good. We went to see the shop, which was nice and large with big rooms above, and we decided to make an offer for it. We decided with our catering experience we would open a restaurant and applied for the necessary planning permission. When the owner of the shop next door heard about this he contacted us. His shop was a snack bar but he had already applied for and got, planning permission to convert it into a licensed restaurant. As this would mean less effort for us we agreed to buy his shop instead. Straight away we put the house on the market thinking we might get about £30,000 but all the agents said £37,000. Vincent decided it should be £39,000 so we agreed at that. We received lots of offers but no one was in a position to act quickly enough for the seller of the café. He was anxious to confirm his sale as he had agreed to buy a clothes shop in Wimbledon. I had a small account with Barclays Bank in the Strand and approached them for a bridging loan. The Manager was extremely helpful and after visiting the shop and seeing us both together he was in favour of the idea and easily agreed to the loan. This was at a time when restaurants were opening rapidly and making lots of money. We all assumed, wrongly, that if the expected Conservative government had power it would mean even bigger things for us all. Soon after we received the bridging loan we were able to sell the house for £41,000 to an advertising man who liked the house as much as we did. If we could have kept both the shop and the house we would have, but I felt sure that within two years we would be able to buy an even better house. After about three months dealing with the building contractors, all the changes were done and we were ready to open. We had a bad start to the business however as Vincent insisted that we only sell English food. I thought we needed more than that to encourage interest in the restaurant but he was insistent saying, "I don't want those black people in here." I tried to reason with him pointing out that Chinese restaurants weren't full of Chinese or the Italians full of just Italians but that it was white people who patronised them. We had applied for a drinks licence in Vincent's name (at his insistence) and planned to sell drinks on our opening night. Just before the application was heard we learnt that the Police were opposing the granting of a licence on the grounds of Vincent's conviction. This didn't surprise me and we made another application in my name but they still opposed, saying that I was totally under Vincent's control. That was no secret but what shocked me was to hear them read out details of another conviction, this one for soliciting, I hadn't known about this and it had happened in the North of England somewhere where I didn't think Vincent had even heard about not less been to. While I had been busy at work Vincent had been roaming, for what and with whom? Just for excitement maybe, it wasn't central to the issue so we never discussed it. The Magistrates hearing was on the morning of the 6th of April 1979 and we had invited everyone to the opening that same night. As we didn't have a licence we gave everybody free alcohol and it was assumed that we had been refused the licence because of Vincent's colour; this was a convenient thought and we let it stay, I was unwilling to discuss 'convictions' with anyone, I planned this as a new start wanting to look forward not backwards. We had to get a specialist solicitor dealing with alcohol licences and appealed against the decision. After 4 months we appeared before a Judge at the Crown Court in Richmond. A counsel represented the Magistrates, the police had a counsel and we had a counsel. The Judge listened to the police counsel and allowed him to question me. When my counsel stood up to speak the Judge adjourned the court saying, "Please wait, I think we can settle this quickly." When he returned into the court he announced that he would approve my application and that there had been no reason for the delay in granting me the licence.

Something about the whole process made it difficult not to believe that Vincent's colour had nothing to do with the delay, after all the same day that I had applied at the Magistrates Court licences were given freely to a man previously convicted of selling stolen liquor, a woman who was going to have her bar in one room and the food in another – this at a time when restaurant licences were very strictly controlled – drinks were only to be served with food. Another man was told that although he had been keeping food on a dirty floor he would get his licence. However it was no all right and we could go back to the restaurant and open up the bar at last. When I said to Vincent how pleased I was he said, "You know there was someone in that court that I recognised, we met late one night – that's what made it easier this time." I thought that once we were granted the licence it would make a big difference to our sales but it didn't. We muddled along until Vincent went to Guyana. Although I did some advertising and we had a good response, when clients came along they had to wait a long time as Vincent would make no advance preparations. "If they can't wait tell them to go" was his constant cry. He lived in a fantasy world and as long as I worked and was able to pay the bills he knew he didn't have to bother too much. I tried to change my duties every week so that I worked in the middle of the day. This enabled me to clean the restaurant in the mornings, do a little shopping and then after work I would plunge straight in and start serving as soon as I got home, or at least I did when anyone was there to be served. Some night we didn't have any customers, it was very depressing for me and I tried to think of a way that we could make things better. Each time I suggested an improvement Vincent found some way of dissuading me. "Everything will work out alright," he said and then we would be in bed and I would forget all about the problems of the day. Although we never made enough money from the restaurant to pay our way we managed to keep going as I had my salary from British Telecom which I managed to keep high by working double shifts on Sundays and even on Christmas Day I would work a double shift. British Telecom arranged taxis for us and they were always late on Christmas mornings. This meant that before I left for the office I could prepare the vegetables and slice the meats for the booked lunches. All Vincent had to do was the actual serving; sometimes I was even able to do that if the taxi didn't come for me. The fact that I had rung in to report meant that I wouldn't lose my money. Even when I reached the office it wasn't busy but we had to keep a full staff in case of emergencies, earthquakes or such similar disasters.

The restaurant hadn't been open for long but we did have a few regular customers; one of these was a rough looking man, a little brutish in appearance but with an engaging smile. He always came with the same lady friend and I got to like them a lot, they were easy to serve and friendly. Before we had our drinks licence they would bring their own bottles of wine, I always gave them an ice bucket and tried to treat them well. Vincent was most outraged that I should treat them so well when it wasn't even our wine that they drank. "Who do they think they are?" he would exclaim from the kitchen. Although he was a marvellous cook he didn't like being in the kitchen.

I tried to persuade him that he should be there until we had established ourselves and then when we could do better we could get someone for him to train. Eventually Vincent taught me some of his culinary secrets and I spent as much time, or more, in the kitchen as I did in front of the restaurant. This particular customer turned out to be the Deputy High Commissioner for Guyana, as soon as Vincent learnt this and being the snob that he was he became much more friendly towards the man. Gradually Vincent and Burgess, who came from the Georgetown suburb of Kitty where he told me he was known as The Beast of Kitty, became firm friends. On one of Prime Minister Burnhams visits to London Burgess suggested to us, "Why not provide food for your leader?" This had not been suggested before and I was all in favour of it having been an admirer of Mr. Burnham for many years and I knew he was one of Vincent's idols. It was arranged that we prepare and deliver a dinner for Mr. Burnham and all the members of his staff at the Knightsbridge Hotel. It was exciting to know that we were cooking for a head of state. We closed the restaurant for the day so that we could concentrate on the preparation and cooking of the typical Creole food of Guyana that Mr. Burnham loved. Later I was to hear many stories from his opponents of his extravagances but from my personal knowledge he was a man who liked a simple life and even in London where he could have eaten anywhere he preferred what he called "Good home food." On that first day Vincent took the food to the hotel and I stayed behind in the restaurant. Mr. Burnham was staying in the Hotel in Knightsbridge leaving the official residence in Lowndes Square in the occupation of the High Commissioner. Vincent escorted the food to the suite where the Guyana High Commission officials wanted him to leave it, but Vincent insisted on staying to serve Mr. Burnham himself, we had discussed this and agreed that there should be no third party between our food and the Prime Minister. When Mr. Burnham saw Vincent he threw his arms around him saying, "Boy! Is that really you, how's your uncle?" They were soon deep in conversation about the old days in Georgetown when Burnham had yet to reach his present status, Walter together with the whole Butters family had supported him and even sheltered him at a difficult time when the British were still in control and Burnham was considered a threat to them. After that visit whenever Mr.Burnham came to London we always provided food for him. Even though we both would have been happy to do this for nothing he insisted each time that we present our bill without delay and payment was always prompt.

As President, Burnham came to London to attend Prince Charles' wedding, he came in style bringing a large entourage that we catered for. Even on the night of the official banquet at Buckingham Palace we were asked to feed President Burnham and his wife as "I can't enjoy the food they serve at those things," said the President. He was aware of how much we both admired him, when the plane flew direct to Guyana we supplied the food for his return journey, "Put your bill in before I leave the country," he would say "Don't let anyone have a chance to forget you are owed this money boy, you know you have to live." We were additionally honoured throughout the following years, when Mrs. Burnham accompanied her husband she would come to Clapham High Street to spend the day with Vincent and I. After lunch Mrs. Burnham and Vincent would go shopping for small items that she wished to take back with her. Mrs. Burnham, known universally in Guyana as Comrade Vi, was a most gracious first lady; she liked to meet all our staff and would remember them by name years afterwards, even if she had met them once only. Just two weeks before President Burnham died, Mrs. Burnham hosted a dinner party at the restaurant for a group of friends, all ladies. Rather than close the restaurant which she did not wish, we arranged her table in one half of the restaurant leaving the other half for regular clients. It was a perfect evening, apart from Mrs. Burnham's party there was a large group of young Guyanese on holiday from North America and so the atmosphere was totally Guyanese. I had prepared a large snapper that had been brought for us from Guyana and made two choices for dessert, one a light sponge decorated with cherries and chocolate and a mousse lightly flavoured with almond and coloured an extremely gentle shade of violet to compliment Mrs. Burnham's first name. Mrs. Burnham, Vincent and I planned that when the Burnham family were next in London together we would have a large celebration at the restaurant. But it wasn't to be, Vincent and I were in the middle of discussing what we might do to ensure that President Burnham would be pleased when the telephone brought us the sad and traumatic news that the President had died while undergoing some minor surgery at Georgetown Hospital. Whatever else passed between Vincent and I, one thing was certain, that was our deep love and admiration for President Burnham. The restaurant was always a place of music but as soon as the news came I turned off the music and no more was played until after the funeral. The restaurant telephone rang constantly as the Guyanese community in London knew that this was the one place in London that belonged spiritually to the President. From early evening until 6am the next day the telephone rang and the restaurant filled with people as if by being in the place where he was truly loved they would be closer to him. Strong men cried and the older men talked of how the President's efforts on behalf of the Guyanese people had changed their lives. The Burnham family called for Vincent to attend the funeral and he went, travelling first class and was treated royally when he arrived in Guyana, of course Clive Lloyd the cricketer went as well, another of Guyana's favourite sons. The constitution of Guyana provided for an immediate transition of the Presidency to the Vice President and Desmond Hoyte took over. When President Desmond Hoyte was duly elected as President Vincent was in his first honours list and received the Medal of Service.

CHAPTER THIRTEEN.

We had only been open for about nine months when Vincent had to go to Guyana to deal with a family problem. I don't know where the money came from, as we certainly didn't make enough in the restaurant. As always my first thought was the old thing but I searched the building from top to bottom but found no trace of any medical bits and pieces so assumed that he had borrowed the money for the fare.

While he was away in Guyana things happened.

Firstly, I persuaded Ruth to come and help me in the kitchen. Together we composed a menu of Guyanese favourites. Pepperpot, Bora Pork, Bolonger Beef, Garlic Pork, Fried Fish, Cook-up Rice, Roti and Curry and a dish really from Jamaica, Salt Mackerel with Green Bananas and Dumplings. The change of menu proved successful and by the time Vincent got back from Guyana we had started to get busy, everyone liked this Creole food and the press started to notice us. But other things were happening as well; Vincent had an old school friend, an old rival in fact. This man was a well-known Obeah man who had a large clientele from all races who consulted him on a variety of matters; he was more successful than Vincent had been, maybe because he was a genuine Obeah man. While Vincent was away Carl introduced me to Amyl Nitrate combined with vodka and Special Brew. I would go to his flat after I closed the restaurant and arrive back the next morning no knowing what had happened in between except that I had lots of mysterious bruises and my body ached. I do remember that when Carl was drunk he would lapse into another character sounding like an Austrian, so different to what he was like usually and he told me he had no idea that it happened. At the same time another man came on the scene, it was as if a secret message told them that Vincent was not there. They were probably around all the time but Vincent knew how to censor the telephone and post. Anyway this man came into my life on February 14th, an easy to remember day and I really enjoyed being with him. Lance came to help me in the evenings and then stayed for the night. As he was married we both took it for granted that as soon as Vincent returned from Guyana the affair would end; but he couldn't leave well alone and neither could I. Stupidly thinking that Vincent would be as understanding as I had been in the past, I told him how much I liked Lance and that I would like to see him for a little while longer. What followed was a torrent of recriminations and rows and soon the whole of the community knew that Lance was trying to take Peter away from him. In the middle of this, Vincent telephoned Lance's wife and explained in minute detail just what Peter and Lance were doing so that when Lance went home from work one day the locks had been changed and his wife had taken out an injunction against him forbidding him entry to his home. I tried to keep some semblance of normality in our lives, working and helping to run the restaurant as usual. This was made difficult by Vincent's habit of drinking heavily and then relating the sad tale to any friends who came to the restaurant to eat.

One night Vincent was drinking heavily with a cousin and after the restaurant closed the cousin stayed while they talked about me and my dreadful sins; I hoped by not …..taking notice of them I would be able to go upstairs to sleep but suddenly they were both hitting me, beating me with their fists and kicking me. I passed out, this dramatic gesture stopped them beating and made them worry if I was dead, but on finding out that I was still breathing they just put me on my bed and left me. When I awoke the next day at first I didn't remember what had happened but the pain from the kicking reminded me and when I looked in the mirror it all cam back, my face was a mass of dried blood, blood all over my clothes. I was so outraged that I went down into the restaurant and broke all the glasses, sweeping them together with all the bottles of spirits down onto the floor, I had to do something to release the passion I felt at the thought that Vincent could do so much to hurt me. I went out into the High Street just as I was and took the bus to his cousin in Balham and there with her granddaughters they cleaned me up and fed me, later on escorting me back to the restaurant. Vincent was contrite, but I had had enough, I just went upstairs not talking to him. The next day at work I had to tell my superiors that I had been mugged but my colleagues knew what had happened and one of them, Shem, sent me to see a friend of his who had a flat in Streatham and was looking for someone to share with. When he saw my bruised face he immediately offered me the room, telling me "Your friend can come here whenever you like, it's no problem." I arranged to move in taking my television, my sewing machine, my Indian carpet and my clothes. Vincent was incensed that I was moving away from him. To take my things over to Streatham I had to hire a van and driver, the driver, an Indian man came and Vincent followed us out to the van – spitting at me and shouting loudly at the man, "Don't have anything to do with him, he is no good, he sucks cock and men fuck him," finishing as the van door closed, spitting directly onto my face. I didn't say anything to the driver except to tell him the address and he didn't say anything about it either; but when we had carried the few things up to the flat he said, "I feel very tired now, it's a pity I can't lie down for a minute." I said, "You mean you want to go to bed with me." "That's right I do," he replied. Vincent's graphic description of my activities had enflamed him and he wanted to experience it for himself. "Please, I said "I have enough problems at the moment, I cannot help you, please go." I sometimes wonder if I shouldn't have done my bit for Anglo-Indian relations at that time but never mind I didn't and that was that.

Lance's wife quickly started divorce proceedings and he decided that we might as well live openly together and he moved into the Streatham flat with me. Although we got on well together I did miss Vincent, in spite of the trauma and the fighting I missed the restaurant and the mix of people I met there. My life away from the restaurant was a bit boring as well. From working all day I had leisure time in the evenings and I didn't know what to do with it. Lance worked shifts and long hours, he spent a lot of time drinking in the pub and coming home late at night very drunk. We carried on for a few months but in my mind I had already forgiven Vincent for the beating and all our friends and relatives stressed that we should be together and forgive each other. Deep down I knew I would go back; Vincent had become part of my life no matter what. Every night I listened for his key in the door and waited to feel the bed shake as his weight fell on it. Whatever was happening now we had experienced our best physical years together and although we were now moving towards more of a brotherhood than a sexual relationship the memory of his strength sexually was a hard yard stick for anyone else to follow.

When Lance and I first became friends he behaved as if I was the most important person in his life. Concerned about my health, my feelings, escorting me across the road, telephoning daily and sometimes hourly. But one of the problems with men, especially Caribbean men is that as soon as they have you safely ensconced in a house, flat or room with them, that is it, you are expected to be busy looking after the house while they go out. It seems as if domesticity should be enough and you should be grateful for the occasional sexual favour, which will have all the hallmarks of being a duty for them. The haircuts, well-pressed suits and money spent switches to someone else and their chase is on again. This happened quickly with Lance and as I didn't have anything to occupy me I felt it more. One night he came home late, drunk as usual and hardly greeting me he telephoned a woman speaking in loving tones. My patience snapped and grabbing the telephone from him I hit him with it. He was too drunk to resist me and when I had finished he fell down in bed bruised and bloody. The next day we agreed that it would be best to separate, I suppose I had already decided to return to Clapham and Vincent was ready to welcome me with open arms. Everything seemed to return to normal but something had changed and I no longer felt the same when we slept together. Vincent's temper got much worse and we were fighting all the time, he was so much stronger than me that I suffered most. I had bites on my arms and chest and was beaten about the head with a large wooden spoon, a hairbrush and a metal pipe. On my visits to the hospital they took no notice once I said that my friend had done it; "Oh a domestic," was the only response. Afterwards Vincent was always so contrite that I forgave him, then one day a Barbadian friend said, "This will lead to something really bad if you let him keep doing that, the next time he wants to fight you why not just go up to your room, lock the door and only come down when he is calmer." I did this, but it made me distance myself from him and we started to sleep in separate rooms and gradually sex diminished to the point of no return. As later events proved, this was a good thing for me. At work I began to hear about a new mysterious disease, apparently sweeping across America, a deadly thing with no cure and no obvious cause. I determined that I would sleep alone and be completely celibate; I knew that Vincent was still having many adventures but I thought that with his medical knowledge he would be careful. When the publicity about this new disease started I was more determined than ever to sleep alone and knowing myself I knew that I had to be completely celibate with no half measures. The Barbadian friend, Sugar, had always been a very good friend to both of us but I began to notice a coolness and felt that she was distancing herself from me. Many years later she told me, "Vincent said you didn't like black people and you especially didn't like me." This was Vincent's way of paying her back for her advice to me. In spite of our problems Vincent was always uppermost in my mind and I know that whatever he did, I was his first thought. Even when we weren't talking our behaviour showed that we were dependent on each other, if one of us had been less wilful things might have been different. I did ask him once if he thought we could have behaved differently, but he answered, "Uh Uh not you and me, we would do the same things exactly, it's just one of those things, you are you and I am me and we cannot change." He had such a hold on me that I compared everyone with him. While I was sexually active I had never found anyone to come up to his standard, maybe it was the same for him and that is why he was so jealous. He always said, "I would trust Peter with a million pounds but not alone in a room with a man."

CHAPTER FOURTEEN.

In 1984 the shop next door had become vacant and Vincent determined that we should buy it. We were still not making money in the original shop but Vincent persuaded me that if we had both shops it would be a big enough restaurant to do large scale catering. As I had always thought it was easier to cater for 200 people that you know are coming than for fifty drifting in at odd times I agreed. Through a contact at the Commission for Racial Equality Vincent was introduced to the Manager of the local National Westminster Bank, they got on well together and a loan went through without even a survey. At the same time I was able to take voluntary redundancy from British Telecom and was able to put £30,000 into the business which we used for the conversion. We were lucky to get an excellent builder; the men came from Reading, arriving each Monday morning, staying until Friday night and slept above the shop. This enabled the work to progress quickly and in two months we were ready to open. We had our opening reception on a bright

Saturday in June. I tried to everything in style, the invitations were on cards with gold edges and turquoise printing, enclosed with the invitation was an acceptance card with a stamped envelope; once again I hoped that this would be yet another new beginning for us. Mr. Joseph the Guyana High Commissioner came with his staff, the Mayor of Lambeth, Pat Williams came and as she was in a wheelchair we had a ramp made for the front door. The Mayor of Lewisham, Les Eytle – a fellow Guyanese, was present with his wife. It was a great occasion; the official cars parked outside made a good focus for the local shoppers. We had prepared an enormous amount of food and only served champagne. I managed to rescue several bottles that staff had hidden by the back door in readiness for their departure but other than that it went without a hitch. As usual I stayed in the background and let Vincent take the bows, he was better at that than at organizing the staff and I felt he was after all an extension of me and any praise given him was automatically given to me as well. After all I had invented 'Butters', that is the public Butters that the world knew. I told everyone that he had all the ideas and explained his slowness by telling people that he wanted everything to be perfect for them. In short I did all I could to boost his image even at the expense of my own, I wanted so much for him to be successful.

The extension of the restaurant failed to make life easier, in fact it proved to be more difficult; we failed to get the amount of large bookings that I had anticipated as we already had the reputation of taking too long to serve and consequently we were passed over in favour of less tasty meals that didn't take so long to serve. Vincent wanted to keep the new section immaculate and hated casual customers to sit there, he was only happy if it was a High Commissioner or other celebrity. This caused many arguments and I regretted leaving British Telecom. Sometime during 1986 Vincent got terribly angry with me over not much at all and together with a friend beat me very badly; when I looked at myself in the mirror I was frightened. I went to the photographer Harry in Landour Road and had some photographs taken which I took to a solicitor in Chancery Lane for advice. His advice was sound but I didn't take it, I knew that I should leave and insist that we sell up but just like any other battered wife I didn't and stayed on. Apart from the hold Vincent had over me there were other things going on that made me stay, earlier that year Vincent had celebrated his 50th birthday; all the Commonwealth High Commissioners came to celebrate with him, amongst the guest were politicians, artists, television personalities, all people that I might not meet otherwise. The Leader of Lambeth Council, Ted Knight, was a frequent visitor, he loved the way Vincent cooked and would stay talking until very late in the night. Ted was very much in the news at the time but I couldn't equate the statements made about him in the press with the unassuming caring person that I knew. Being a part of the Black Community I appreciated the way he actively encouraged black women to take an active part in local politics. Amelda Inyang, Irma Critchlow and then Sharon Atkin came to us immediately after their election to the council to celebrate. When Sharon entered the restaurant in triumph I played my recording of The Calendar Song as loud as possible, it was the most joyful calypso record that I had. When the Lambeth Councillors were taken to court over rate capping we were there in Jubilee Gardens dispensing tea and breakfast to the supporters who marched with the Councillors early in the morning to the High Court. We had met Janet Boateng when she was a councillor and chair of the Lambeth Social Services; through her we met Paul Boateng. Leading up to the general election of 1987 Vincent encouraged Paul and went up to Brent South to canvass for him and was with them on the night of the election. I stayed at home but baked a large three-tiered cake that I iced in white and covered with deep red roses. I stayed awake listening to the election news until I heard that Paul had won his seat and then went to bed. It must have been two or three o'clock when Vincent ran upstairs shouting "Peter wake up, Paul has won, everyone is downstairs – come and celebrate." I went downstairs to the restaurant and presented my cake to Paul who was garlanded with flowers and jumping up and down still excited at his victory. Including Janet and Paul's election agent there were about a dozen people in the restaurant; everyone was hungry so I went into the kitchen and cooked for us all. We ate and drank champagne until 6am when Paul had to leave to prepare for his first television interview as a Member of Parliament. The election had given us three other black MP's, Keith Vaz, Diane Abbot and a Guyanese Bernie Grant. The Sunday after the election was Paul's birthday and with Janet, Vincent and I planned a birthday celebration that would include the new MP's including Ken Livingstone who we all felt was 'one of us'. The restaurant was packed, Paul and Janet's families and their own five children, the last of which Seph was to be Vincent's latest godchild.

But the proudest moment for me was to be introduced to Mrs. Oliver Tambo, wife of the ANC leader, who was a truly dignified lady; stately in her gold cloth with the air of someone who was entirely confident and aware of her position in society.

I had noticed that for the whole of 1987 Vincent had shown signs of discomfort and deep depression, it is difficult to pinpoint exactly when the depression became more than usual. Ever since I first met him he had a habit of just being very quiet when we were alone and when asked he would just say that nothing was wrong except that he had a headache. His headaches were well known in his family and we all accepted that he just didn't want to discuss whatever was on his mind at the time. One day while I was on the telephone talking to my Mother she told me that lately whenever she spoke to Vincent she felt very depressed but wasn't sure why. Vincent liked my mother, but his pride would not let him ask for help in his last big confrontation with life. This was unlike the times when we were arguing and he asked her to pay us a visit in order "To sort Peter out for me." Sometimes he did say that he was holding so many secrets for other people that his head felt as if it would burst not being able to relate them to anyone else. It became increasingly obvious that something different was wrong with him; he drank at least half a bottle of rum each day plus whatever he drank while he was out and he never refused drinks offered by customers and friends in the restaurant. The restaurant wasn't very busy and we were managing with just two students in the kitchen. They were both eager to learn and quickly picked up our style of cooking and service but Vincent behaved as if he hated them and constantly picked fault with them, swearing loudly and abusively so that the whole restaurant was filled with the sound of his raised voice. I knew that if I interfered it would lead to arguments between us that would make the situation worse. I tried to laugh it off but we lost even more customers and when I asked him to tell me why he was behaving like this he just said that there was no reason and why, what did I think was wrong? He just wouldn't relax although I tried very hard to make him calm down; I spoke to all the friends that I thought he trusted and asked them to try and find out for me what was wrong with him. Everyone that I asked was so eager to help, it was so obvious that something was amiss. I asked all kinds of people, Cita Pilgrim, the High Commissioners wife, spent the whole of one Sunday with us, willingly cancelling appointments in an effort to be of help, but we learnt nothing new. An old school friend of his, a chemist Hassan Ally and his wife came but Vincent would not tell him anything at all, I consulted with all his cousins and aunts but we could not think what could be wrong. An older cousin, Priscilla, told me "It must be Taipee." "What's that?" I asked. "That's what we call it in Guyana" she said, "When you are in love Taipee takes three courses, in the first flush of the affair you cannot think, sleep or eat properly because you are thinking of your new love and you are jealous wondering what they are doing all the time. After that you see your lovers face in the food when you go to eat so you can't eat, if the affair continues to go wrong the third stage leads to death." That made some kind of sense to me, he spent hours just looking out of the window and seemed to be waiting for someone or something to happen. I decided to myself that that was it and he would soon snap out of it. But he didn't snap out of it and this state lasted for about a year but he wasn't worse until one afternoon he came to me and said that he didn't feel well, he looked very hot and his tongue was coated and mauve in colour; I called Dr. Adams who came at once and prescribed some drops for his tongue and suggested a thorough check up and gave him a letter to take to the hospital. The next day Vincent left to go to the hospital and when he came home I asked him what had happened. "Oh I couldn't go today, I will go tomorrow." He was out all the next day until the evening and when he came in he said that he had been to the hospital but that they were too busy to make an appointment for him. This went on for a week with varying excuses as to why he hadn't seen anyone at the hospital. I stopped asking him so often and when two months later I asked him if he had been he answered "Oh yes I went and they told me there is nothing wrong with me and I am very well." What could I do, he was an adult and I couldn't force him to do anything he didn't want to do. Gradually Vincent lost all interest in eating, leaving most of the food on the plate. He had always been a great eater loving cakes and chocolates and plenty of rice, if he didn't eat rice three times a day he hadn't eaten at all. He was losing weight rapidly but as he insisted that nothing was wrong with him I thought it's that old Taipee still. By August he was only appearing in the restaurant for about an hour each day. On Sunday and Monday when we were closed he wouldn't get up at all. Worried that he was eating less and less I tried to think of something that would make him want to eat. I bought all the foods that he liked to eat that we didn't buy now like those cake shop trifles, I bought them but he left them untouched, I made soups, Ruth made soups and fried fish, all of which he left. For about three months the only nourishment he would take was a 'Cogue' which is an egg nog made with three eggs beaten with some vanilla essence, a tot of brandy and a pint of warm milk with some sugar all beaten up together. Soon he was staying in bed all the time. In a way it was easier for me downstairs with the restaurant, although I was more or less on my own at least I didn't have the shouting and abusing in the kitchen to explain away to the few customers that we had. Vincent refused to see anyone at all during this time. Hearing that he was unwell Dr. Adams came to the restaurant regularly but Vincent would not see him. Knowing that Vincent was unwell a steady stream of friends and relatives called at the restaurant to see him, most of them bringing food and drink which is the Guyanese custom when visiting someone unwell. I asked him each time to see them but he would get so angry if I tried to insist and I had the hard task of telling them that he would not see them. This went on for about three months and after a cousin travelled across London to see him bringing soup with her and he refused to see her saying "Tell her I am too sick to see anyone." The poor girl cried and was most upset. This was on a Saturday morning and I thought about it for the rest of that day and decided that whatever he said the next visitor that came I would send them up to him no matter what. On Sunday Elma, his cousin's wife, came to see him so I just sent her upstairs to him, I did not go into the room with her but I heard him shout "I can't see you I'm not well." Elma replied, "Well it's me and I'm here so you have to make the best of it." When she had gone I went up to him and he said angrily "You shouldn't have let her come up here you know I don't want to see anyone." I said "Well if you don't want to see them you had better come downstairs and tell them not to come, I cannot turn them away anymore, they will think that I am doing something bad to you that I don't want them to see." After all, I thought 'he says nothing is wrong with him so he could come down and deal with his visitors'. When I related this to Cita and Ruth, they both agreed, Ruth said that people were already asking why Peter was keeping everyone away from Vincent. I didn't want them to stay away; on the contrary, I was on my own and needed help in keeping his room clean. We were doing so badly in the restaurant that I was struggling to do most things myself. I had to shop in the mornings, clean the restaurant and the kitchen and during the afternoon cook the food ready for the night. After Elma had been I showed up everyone that came to visit. They all brought food with them that he didn't eat. "I will eat it later," he told them and then when they had gone he told me to either eat it myself or give it to the cat. I tried to persuade him that he should eat some of the food but he said, "No my chest hurts and I don't want it yet." I had refrigerators full of containers with different dishes in, poached salmon, cook-up-rice, dhal, choka, roti, fried fish and custards but they were all wasted. I couldn't possibly tell the bearers of all this food that it was all going unused. At that time I still had no idea what was wrong with Vincent, thinking all the time that it was just the same depression, not knowing that by this time he was quite ill. If I had been more experienced the condition of his tongue would have told me that he had thrush and then I might have realised that his chest pain was the result of the thrush moving down into his body. But I didn't know then and even thought that he was just using his chest as an excuse, to hide his depression, after all I knew that whenever he had a chest pain in the past his first remedy was Vicks Vapour Rub and as he hadn't used this I thought it was nothing. How could I know that he was past getting benefit from the palliative effects of vapour rub. One of his brothers came from Canada to see him; Vincent asked him, "What do you want? What do you think I have for you?" I didn't interfere, I knew that Vincent had no time for his brother but at least he helped me to clean Vincent's room. Christmas eve night I was left alone with Vincent, he looked too ill then, his skin grey and his breath very shallow, I thought he might die that night, I stood downstairs in the bar drinking rum and crying, I couldn't think what to do, I went back upstairs to look at him and he was sleeping peacefully, his breathing regular and his skin colour back to normal. Peter, I said to myself, he won't die just like that, if he is going to die soon he will wait until his birthday in February, after all his mother died on his birthday and his cousin Carrie died on the 6th of February as well, he will wait until then. Christmas morning and I was busy in the restaurant preparing the Christmas lunches when Dorothy, a friend from the Guyana High Commissioners office, came and brought with her enough food for a feast – roast turkey, pepperpot, ham, beef, vegetables, fruits and wine. I was so sorry that Vincent wouldn't touch any of it while she was there so I told her that he would eat later on, how could I tell her after all her kindness that he wouldn't touch it at all. After the Christmas period I did manage to persuade him to visit the hospital where they started to do tests on him. He wouldn't let me see the doctor with him, so I don't know what he told them, they performed test and test, day after day we trailed all over the labyrinth of St.Thomas hospital going from clinic to clinic. Finally towards the end of January he was admitted to hospital with pneumonia, he was very disagreeable and unpleasant to the nursing staff but by the 6th of February after he had received a blood transfusion he was smiling and eating and chatting to the nurses using all his old charm. "I was a little anaemic, that's all," is what he told me and asked me to bake two cakes for the nursing staff. I thought how grand it is, he will be better now and life will progress again. Over the months there had been a lot of speculation as to the reason for his loss of weight, the obvious thought of most people was AIDS, but I couldn't see what that had to do with Vincent, after all he had just been depressed and not eaten that's why he had gotten so thin. I still didn't know that the thrush had made it too painful for him to eat. As the restaurant was not making enough money for us to pay our way we had remortgaged earlier so that the roof could be renewed and the rooms upstairs renovated so that we could get an income from them. I had planned that each room would have it's own shower and toilet. When the roof was done we had asked a Guyanese builder to do the rooms. The price we agreed on seemed fair but when I realised that he had done less than half the works promised and used three quarters of the money something was wrong. We told him not to continue and the money left from the remortgage was soon used up making the monthly repayments and soon we had no money at all. I had to shop daily, carrying all the food myself as we had no paid staff. Ruth came in the evenings to help me, I couldn't even pay her fares, I used my Barclaycard to buy wine and a store card to buy gateaux, I was soon heavily in debt there and the cards were cancelled. I spent many hours wondering what on earth I could do now, after much thought and visiting auctions and estate agents I figured that we could either sell the whole premises or lease the restaurant out and live upstairs. Further along the High Street Mr. Singh had done this with his supermarket and it seemed to be a good idea. The effects of the transfusion on Vincent didn't last and he soon contracted pneumonia again, when he came our of hospital this time he was extremely depressed but still insisting that there was nothing much wrong with him. His leg muscles didn't work properly but I thought that it was just the result of lying in bed for so long and tried to get him to exercise. When we went back to the hospital, I had assumed from what Vincent said that it was for more tests, as according to him they still didn't know what was wrong with him. We entered the waiting room of the special clinic and was struck by the friendliness of the reception, the offer of coffee and biscuits, all so different to the usual detached attitude of hospital staff. The walls of the waiting room were covered with posters cautioning Safer Sex, Use Clean Needles, and Counselling Centres. The majority of the patients waiting to see the doctor were male and it crossed my mind 'could it be? – Was it possible?' No I decided, don't be silly; this doctor is probably a blood specialist that's why we are here, nothing sinister about that, this is probably the most convenient clinic for him to work in that's all. Vincent saw the doctor, as usual alone, and came out saying that he had to have more tests done; we spent the rest of the day in the hospital once again visiting several clinics. My fears for Vincent were allayed, it was obvious that they didn't know yet what was wrong. Allayed that is until the next morning when I investigated his medicines and found that he had been given AZT. A chill struck me and I felt as if my stomach had disappeared, my neck felt rigid, I looked at Vincent lying there on the bed looking so lost and lonely, no words seemed appropriate. I busied myself preparing some scrambled eggs for him, hoping that he would eat. At that time I had no idea of the progression of the infection, I had read that persons diagnosed HIV positive could live from ten to fifteen years, surely in ten years time some treatment would have been found. If I could look after him for a few years everything would be alright. Like most people I had put the thought of this infection away from me and not knowing that the disease had progressed in Vincent long past the stage where ten years were possible; for the past three years at least his symptoms had gone untreated because he wouldn't seek help, being too conscious of how some people would gossip and wishing somehow to save face he had allowed the disease to progress making it difficult to overcome the infections that were now raiding his body. Even in his sick state something else had him pre-occupied. I suggested that a solution to our money problems could be to lease half the restaurant keeping the original shop and both upper parts. Making enquiries I found that we could obtain a large enough premium to pay off our mortgage arrears and finish the rooms upstairs with monthly rentals enough to pay our outgoings, which would mean that anything we made in the restaurant would be ours. Thinking that Vincent wouldn't be able to work in the restaurant for a while I was sure that I could continue to run a smaller restaurant with ease. I soon found a prospective tenant willing to pay the premium that I asked for and the rental as well. The man, an Italian, and his partner were going to install a kitchen behind the shop spending at least £20,000 on it. With an upward rent review every four years it seemed perfect. They produced plans for our approval, Vincent opposed each one, he wasn't keen on letting anyone open another restaurant next to us, I tried to convince him that it was different anyway and we would be getting rent from it as well. To no avail, he refused to agree to my plan and then announced that he wanted to sell up everything so that he could return to Guyana. I tried to dissuade him from this; the fear of disease is bad enough in England but the prejudice even against a common cold is more in the Caribbean. "How can you think of that?" I asked him, "What about medicine, it costs thousands a year." He replied that he had many friends in Guyana who would be able to help him and was adamant that we sell. There was nothing I could say to convince him that it was the wrong thing to do, he just wouldn't listen. Each day he was visited by his cousin Mr. Caesar and a young man Patrick Whall, the son of some Guyanese friends. They held long conversations with Vincent, being silent and glaring at me when I went near to them. I was in a state of complete confusion, the strain of the past years had left me unable to cope with this sudden development. Dr. Adams gave me a course of tranquillisers, I concluded that if Vincent did want to sell then I couldn't stop him and I began to look forward to doing something else with my life. Vincent made it very clear that I had no part in his plans for his future. We agreed to sell, Vincent told me that he had asked an agent in Streatham to sell the shop and I asked another one. When my agent wanted to bring a prospective buyer Vincent said that he had already agreed a sale but he couldn't remember the name of the person who he said was making a direct offer to Mr. Hill the solicitor. Mr. Hill did receive an offer from a firm called 'Rose' for £400,000 but then my agents client offered £435,000, which was obviously better. At this offer Vincent became extremely agitated, shouting and swearing at me he said, "Just because it's an Italian you want to sell to him so that you can have sex with him." This was the last thing on my mind, I just thought that an extra £35,000 was worth thinking about but Vincent insisted that 'Rose' was going to pay cash and the sale would be quick. I asked my agent to send the offer in writing anyway but I didn't get any mail at all. This all turned out to have been just a scheme to get rid of me, after all these years and all we had been through, for some reason which I never found out Vincent was prepared to lose me forever. What was in his mind and what thoughts had been given to him I will never know. When I found out from Mr. Hill that Vincent was one of the purchasers and then from Patrick that he was to be the other partner I was stunned at the deception. Patrick put such a good case to me that he would be helping Vincent and that I could stay upstairs and live there for as long as I wished. Patrick told me that 'Rose' was one of his companies. I did go to companies house out of curiosity to check and found that although there was a 'Rose' the company had nothing to do with Patrick and was still trading and entering accounts but by this time I was tired and wanted to settle things as quickly as possible; the outstanding mortgage and other bills worried me. I worked out what my share would be if we made a sale for £400,000 and began to search for a house of my own to buy. Vincent and Patrick obtained a mortgage but were only able to pay me £100,000 promising to pay the other £40,000 within six months. My solicitor drew up a second charge for me and I agreed to this as property prices were rising daily and I felt secure that the money would be there. If I had been more aware and not under sedation I might have found it more strange that Patrick was using his Grandmother's name Aaron and not his father's name Whall. Patrick continued to be the thoughtful caring person that I had know for the past ten years, or so it appeared. Vincent, once he had obtained his wish to keep the restaurant whole at any cost, was more amenable and friendly. I decided to stay above the restaurant until I received the remaining £40,000. I had already seen a house in Streatham that I liked a lot and thought it would be suitable for fostering children. There was plenty of time I thought as Vincent wanted me to stay as long as possible, I was in no hurry now that I was no longer responsible for the debts and felt more relaxed. When we went to Mr. Hill to sign the papers for the sale of the restaurant to Vincent and Patrick, Vincent suddenly looked at me with the old look and asked me what we were doing, I said to him that this was just like a divorce but somehow it wasn't really – just another phase in our relationship. Vincent was still weak but I thought that he would improve, still not realising just how far the disease had progressed. It is possible then that I could have persuaded Vincent to stop the change of ownership to Vincent and Patrick but I had had enough of the worries accompanying the business and Vincent was still insistent that the restaurant should not be leased out. I had decided to go ahead with the purchase of the house in Streatham as soon as I got the balance of the £40,000 from them but in the meantime agreed to stay on and even said that I would be willing to work in the restaurant when they re-opened it. Vincent was pleased and insisted that he would soon be well and then everything would go on as before in the restaurant. Patrick waiting for some time and then got restless. By November he was beginning to change his ways, no longer playing the part of a trusted younger man he became bullyish towards me and then on the 10th November went into the room where Vincent was in bed and shouted at him for a long time, mainly he was upset because "I'm getting nothing out of this, Peter has got £100,000 and I have got nothing." I thought this was strange as I assumed that he would be bringing something into the business not just joining Vincent to take something out. I came to the conclusion, that in common with many people, Patrick had assumed that the business was making money and that Vincent would be able to be generous to him. The Berlin wall came down on the 11th and down as well came Patrick's pretence of niceness. Because I had told a friend Beverly on the Saturday when she came to see Vincent just how I had been weaselled out of the business and that I couldn't move because I still hadn't got all my money from them, Patrick threatened me with violence if I talked to anyone else about our business affairs. He threatened to bring in one of his uncles and he knew that I didn't like that particular uncle who was a violent man. Patrick referred to the time when the uncle came to the restaurant in a violent mood wanting to beat me up on Vincent's behalf. To hide the fact that he had very bad thrush, Vincent answering questions as to the state of his mouth apparently told someone that his mouth was bad because I had beaten him. When the uncle came and shouted at me I tried not to be involved because I knew by then the reason for Vincent's wishing to hide the truth and he had blamed me before in the past when wishing to escape trouble. I realised that with Patrick's attitude I would not be able to stay at the restaurant once I had got all the money due to me. Vincent was getting weaker not stronger and I thought it was largely due to the strain of Patrick's behaviour. Vincent had ordered a case of rum from a man who travelled between Guyana and London so that they would have real Guyanese rum for when they re-opened. Patrick had said that he would pay for this but was unable to and the man had to take the rum back. Vincent was obviously worried saying, "My Mother told me that when you run away from Jumbie you fall into the coffin." I knew that he meant that I was the Jumbie or ghost and he regretted running away from me. On Wednesday the 22nd of November Vincent had an appointment at the hospital, for some test he said, but when Wednesday morning came he asked me to telephone the hospital to say that he was too sick to go. I told him that the hospital was the place to go if he was sick. He asked me to go with him but I said that I wouldn't if I just had to sit in the corridor like a stranger. He asked me why as I knew what was wrong with him; I said that if the doctor didn't know me and just what our relationship was they wouldn't tell me anything even if he died. He agreed that this time he would let me talk to the doctor. When we got to the hospital he couldn't walk in and we had to use a wheelchair to get up to the clinic. I had met his doctor before when I had gone to the hospital to try and get some help, although they couldn't let me know the true state of Vincent's health they had helped me through counselling and I had began to accept what was happening. This time the doctor was happy to see me, he told Vincent that he had a small infection in his chest and he would admit him for a few days and that as Vincent was so weak he would like to send him to a respite centre like the Mildmay or the Lighthouse for a few weeks. Vincent was horrified at the suggestion that he would go into an institution that was so obviously for people suffering from AIDS and said no he wanted to go back home and that Peter would look after him. Even after the torments of the summer and the way he had inveigled me out I couldn't refuse; feelings of love and tenderness filled me and I would willingly have changed places with him then. I said of course I would look after him and furthermore if my house was ready and he was still not well I would take him there and look after him for as long as was necessary. After I had seen him settled into the ward I left and went home. Waiting in the High Street for me was Mr. Clark whose wife, Elizabeth, had been my good friend; we visited each other regularly but earlier in the summer she had been taken ill and been in the hospital in Landor Road. Mr. Clark had come to tell me that Elizabeth had died and that her funeral would be on Monday. I went to see Vincent each day, when I got back on Sunday from a visit Patrick was standing down in the restaurant. "We have been burgled" he said, "I have called the police and they will be here soon." I went upstairs to my room, the door had been broken and the room ransacked, all my rings, my gold bracelet, the gold plated cutlery that we had only used once when President Hoyte had visited us, video recorder, passport, drivers licence, everything of value. Nothing else had been taken from any other part of the building. Apparently the thieves had got in through the window leading on to the flat roof at the front. Once I would have been very upset at this, but I knew I was insured and besides I had more to worry about. Elizabeth was to be buried the next day and Vincent was sick in hospital. He developed a large swelling over one eye, to try and get rid of the infection quickly the doctors decided to operate and drain the fluid away. I waited all day for him to come out of the anaesthetic, he looked so poorly then and even when he awoke properly he was very drowsy in his manner. I went to the hospital each day at 9-30am and didn't leave until 10pm. I helped the nurses to clean him as he had become incontinent and I tried to feed him, as he had no interest in food. He had no other visitors at this stage, the ones that might have come he had told not to visit him and the others were overcome by superstition. Although, myself, I had no fear of infection from the everyday case of a sick person I could understand the fears as a year ago I had been full of such fears myself. By facing up to the manner of this infection it had lost its terrors for me. The nurses at St. Thomas hospital treated Vincent with such respect and kindness and because they knew of our relationship treating me with care as well. I still didn't know enough about the disease to know that this was going to be Vincent's last few weeks. Still thinking of the 10 to 15 years that I imagined still awaited him, I looked forward to nursing him at home and then moving with him to Streatham. On the 11th December the hospital decided that Vincent could come home. I was prepared for him, the District Nursing Service had provided me with a special mattress to help prevent bedsores and I had a good supply of everything necessary to nurse him. "Thank God I am home with you," he whispered to me, "If you hadn't said you would look after me I don't know what I would have done." "Who else would look after you but me" I smiled at him. The first night home Vincent fell asleep quickly, tired out by the transfer from the hospital. The next day the District Nurse came to help me wash him and look at the bedsores which had appeared as if by magic. I had always thought a bedsore would be like a rash, I wasn't prepared for the burn like wounds that appeared on his flesh. For the next two days Vincent was just sleepy, his eye was still painful from the operation. But then by Thursday morning he was able to open his eyes fully and started to take notice of his surroundings. I was able to show him the Christmas cards we had received which were nothing like the usual amount, only one or two. For a while in the morning he sat in an armchair, he said he didn't want anything to eat; I was relieved in a way as Patrick had put a lock on the kitchen door and I couldn't get in to cook anything. I had a supply of high calorie drinks that I persuaded Vincent to drink. It was not until late in the afternoon that someone was in the kitchen and made a little cornmeal porridge for me to give him. Patrick was behaving very peculiarly, suspicious and paranoic as if I was doing something wrong to him. When Vincent is well I thought he will sort everything out. Shortly after that while I was still trying to get him to accept a little of the cornmeal, the door opened and there was his brother Cedric together with Mr. Caesar. They had decided to call Cedric from Canada but had not told me anything about it. If it had been left to me I wouldn't have encouraged Cedric to come, Vincent had no great love for this brother and when he appeared Vincent immediately turned his head to the wall and refused to speak to him, closing his eyes and feigning sleep until Cedric had left the room. "Why is he here?" he asked me, "I don't know Vincent, I certainly didn't call him or know that he was coming." Later that night I read to him from a book of poems, mostly about love. One that I liked was about a young man asking how, if his mother and father slept alone in two cold beds, how did he come into existence. "That sounds like us doesn't it?" I asked Vincent, "Hum" he muttered, and I asked him "If we could do it all again do you think we would be different?" "Uh uh, not you and me, we would do exactly the same things again, you are you and I am I and that's that." For the first time in ages we cuddled and I spent the night sleeping next to him. I had the feeling that when he was better we would be able to resume a more loving relationship again. But it was not to be, for two days Friday and Saturday he suffered the most appalling headaches, "Peter I know that you couldn't bear this pain and I pray that you never get to this." I stayed with him the whole time, it was hard knowing that the other three men in the building were busy searching everywhere, hoping to find his will or his jewellery. What importance could they attach to that when he was in so much pain, but I still didn't realise that he was dying and still looked forward to the time when he could take charge again. On Saturday morning the doctor prescribed a strong pain killer for him, when I had been to the chemist he took them and getting relief from his headache fell into a calm sleep. Good, I thought, after a good nights sleep he will feel better tomorrow. I watched him sleeping; he looked so much better, his face unlined, his skin clear and bright his breathing regular. I didn't believe that he would die, at least not before me. I had convinced myself that he was getting better, after all he looked better and he was showing more interest than he had for ages. Oh yes, I'm told now, people always look like that just before it happens; but how would I have known that? I had no experience of death and hadn't he always told me and I believed him that wherever I was and whoever I was with and I died he would find me and while I was still warm he would fuck me and be the last man to have sex with me before I was buried. He told me this often and always with such conviction that I did believe him. Even now it would not surprise me, I even look forward to it. When I am dying or just beyond the point of life, Vincent will come for me and together we will make love into the beyond and nothing will separate us. We never did have a tranquil relationship but it lasted for 28 years, turmoil from start to finish, surprises all the way and a life more enriched than I would have had with any other man. To say that we were made for each other may seem fanciful, but anyone that ever knew us will only be able to think of us together. Early on Sunday morning, about 6am it started to rain heavily, I drank some water and dozed off until about 9-30am when I got up to start the day. Vincent was showing signs of movement but a bit drowsy; I decided it was due to the pain killers but when they wear off a bit I would try to get something for him to eat. I got some warm water from the bathroom and bathed his eyes and used small sponges to clean his mouth of some of the thrush and mucus that had collected during the night. All the while I was talking quietly to him, about the weather and other trivia so that he would feel comforted in the ordinariness of things. Then just after 10am I said that I would get some nice hot water ready so that when the nurse came we could bathe him and freshen him up so that he would be ready if any visitors called. I turned away and on reaching the door turned back just in time to see him gently take his last breath and then stop breathing. I knew he had died but I needed confirmation and asked him if that was it, was he sure? I held him and kissed him, his body warm and soft but so very still; I looked at the clock and saw it was 10-30, I asked him again if he was really sure that this was it, I felt he might change his mind and come back. For so many years he had told me what to do and now he wasn't telling me what to do and I felt strange to be deciding for myself. I called the doctor and the nurse and went back beside him to wait. Patrick came in soon after that and started to telephone most of the names in my telephone book so that everyone would know, the news soon spread and the telephone was busy with people calling us to confirm that it was true. When the nurse came we washed him for the last time and dressed his bedsores, now that he was dead he was easy to move about but I cradled his head so as not to make it ache and talked to him as if he knew what we were doing. I had already arranged through Jan Wolf the HIV co-ordinator for Lambeth that Ashtons funeral parlour would handle the funeral, the nurse contacted them and I sat down beside Vincent to wait for them to come. I kissed Vincent often and talked to him, when Cedric came he gave just a quick look and then went with Mr. Caesar to continue his search of the building as if we weren't there. As soon as the undertaker came and Vincent was gone Patrick turned to me with his face full of hatred and said why didn't I leave now as there was nothing for me now. I said where would I go, as I had nowhere to stay, Cedric intervened and Patrick ungraciously relented and I stayed. When they had gone one of the nurses who had attended Vincent on Friday evening came to give me her condolences and warned me against Cedric, he had asked her if she knew where Vincent had put his will, this had shocked her as that was the first time she had seen Vincent; I had seen Cedric talking to her but had assumed that he was making enquiries about his brothers health not his will. Vincent would not have been surprised, once again confirming his ability to understand people. As soon as I was alone in the building I lit a candle for Vincent and leaving it burning went out to the 'Two Brewers' further along the High Street so that I could hear noisy music, drink cold lager and make sure that life was still going on. On Monday morning a good friend Victor called and together with Patrick and Cedric we went to Ashtons to arrange the funeral. I was determined no matter what, I would do exactly what I knew Vincent wished. Victor had been well instructed by Vincent who had told him a year before that he wished to be buried and not cremated and that the undertaker must be Ashtons. As Cedric was returning to Canada on Friday I suggested that we could have the funeral on Thursday, which would be the last available day before the Christmas holidays, I didn't want to leave everything waiting until the New Year. We looked at the catalogue of coffins, only one appealed to me and Cedric agreed, it was a dark oak one. When Cedric asked if it was possible to see one of the coffins the arranger led us into another room so that we could see the variety of coffins. As soon as we went into the room I saw The One and said that is it. It was a large dark wood coffin with the last supper engraved on it in relief on both sides, the top was carved and the baroque brass handles were just one step from being too large and I knew that this was the one Vincent would have chosen for himself. Through the undertakers we arranged to hold the service at the Holy Trinity church on Clapham Common. The two days before the funeral passed in a dark haze, I tried to keep out of Patrick's way, I was afraid of his sudden changes of mood and wanted to keep some control of the funeral otherwise it might not have been what Vincent had wished. I asked Sybil Phoenix of the Marsha Phoenix Trust, a home for girls, if she would prepare a programme of hymns showing the order of service and if she, a Methodist preacher, could arrange with the Vicar of Holy Trinity to take part in the service and speak about Vincent. This was the best thing for me to do, as the time came up for the funeral Patrick tried to usurp my position by claiming to be a nephew of

Vincent, making my position less than it was and somehow I think wanting to put himself up as part of the family so that he could claim some share of Vincent's estate. When we reached the church, family and friends who resented Patrick's behaviour made sure that I sat in the first place at the front. I asked the High Commissioner for Guyana to sit beside me, as Vincent would have wished. My position was made even clearer as soon as Mrs. Phoenix spoke, she told of Vincent's life as a child and young man, she spoke of Vincent's arrival in England when the phrase 'Vincent and Peter' rang clear and true and the whole congregation nodded their approval. Vincent's coffin stood open so that we could all pay our last respects, I had been to the funeral parlour and dressed him in his white dinner jacket and pinned his medal of service on to it, I gave him his favourite slippers and surrounded him with red roses. The procession of mourners started, I went up first to the coffin and kissed Vincent, then down round the foot of the coffin and back to look once more and kiss him again. I went back to my seat and the congregation after looking at Vincent came down to me and without exception embraced and kissed me. All the time I was thinking just how much Vincent would have been pleased with the amount of people that had come to his funeral with only three days notice, he would have been especially pleased that among the congregation were famous sportsmen, actors, politicians and representatives from all the Commonwealth High Commissions. We took him on his last journey to West Norwood Cemetery, luckily, because it was muddy, the plot was on the edge of the path and not too far inside the grounds. I took my turn in filling in the grave with the muddy clay and when the Vicar had completed the service we stayed and sang hymns until the earth had been piled up on top of him and the flowers arranged over the mound. Back at the restaurant I felt ashamed that I could not offer the hospitality that I would have wished to do. Patrick, trying to assume the mantle of chief mourner, had said that he would provide food and drink. The amount of food he prepared for hundreds was more like I would have prepared for six people. Most people had become aware of the situation and knew that I had no access to the kitchen and left quickly as there was no alcohol and such little food and Patrick's insistence that he was a relative made them uneasy as to his intentions. Once again when most of the people had gone he asked me to leave, I knew that I had the right to stay there and resisted him. One of his girlfriends, a white girl, talked to him and he agreed to give me a key to the door, as he would not be there over the Christmas weekend. Patrick had changed all the locks in the building and my room door was still broken, the only room that I had access to that had a lock was the room Vincent had been in and I slept there, using the same sheets and pillows as it was comforting to feel his presence on them.

CHAPTER FIFTEEN.

I spent Christmas day with Ruth and her sister, starting with breakfast at Ruth's house where I had a typical Guyanese Christmas morning breakfast, Pepperpot, Garlic Pork and fresh Creole bread. Then on to Clem to watch his children open up their presents and for the adults to start drinking. It was ten o'clock in the morning and Ruth's sister Winnie was already drunk saying that she was just happy to know that with God's help I have reached another year. Well no arguing with that I thought, then on to Ruth's niece Colleen for dinner that lasted until midnight. Colleen never has done things by halves and gave us four starters including a hot one made with Avocado and then a main course that made the starters look like nothing. By the time I got back to the restaurant I was ready to sleep. Patrick came on Boxing Day morning and apologised for his previous behaviour. I tried to understand him, thinking that he was upset because he was confused about Vincent. We agreed that we should talk together as we were the only ones really concerned with the restaurant and Vincent's affairs. Himself as part owner of the premises and myself as previous owner of the business and still at least half owner of all the contents of the building. I felt better about the situation and agreed to help him all I could. Two days later I had arranged to go to the Commonwealth Institute with Patra Fernando, a good friend to both Vincent and myself. We were to see Doris Harper-Wills interpretation of Caribbean Christmas stories. I got ready early and went up to Clapham Common to visit Winifred, a lady in her nineties that I had come to know while shopping in the High Street. Winifred wasn't in, I went back to the restaurant and chaos reigned. Patrick was there with another man who sometimes worked for him, another man was changing the locks once again. I went to the room behind the restaurant where I had been sleeping to take off my coat; the room was in a mess, all the chairs had been turned upside down and the bed as well. Patrick rushed at me, in one hand a bunch of papers and in the other hand a silver coloured chopper that had been in a cupboard. A rush of words came out of Patrick. "You and Vincent have been plotting against me, you think I am stupid but I'm not, I know what's going on." Mystified I asked him what he meant, but he shouted at me that I shouldn't say anything as all I did was to say bad things about him. I tried to say that I still did not know what was wrong but he threatened me with the chopper, raising it above his head. I sat down on the bench seat in the restaurant and then the other man said that he wanted to punch me as I didn't like black people and that he was black. This was a nightmare, it was all so unreal, Patrick had changed, like Jekyl and Hyde he had two personalities and the other man could only be mad. How could anyone accuse me of not liking black people when black people were the only people I had lived with for 28 years and as far as I knew I had black ancestry as well. Patrick waved one of the papers in front of my face, it was a letter from the estate agents addressed to me but which I had never received. It offered £435,000 for the restaurant and had been intercepted by Vincent who hid it so that I would agree to accept the figure of £400,000. I was the wronged and injured party but Patrick had twisted it in his mind that it mean that I was up to something devious. I was stunned; each time I tried to talk to him he raised the chopper above his head as if to hit me with it and then brought it down, breaking glasses and hacking at the pictures on the wall in his frustration. What could I do, there was nobody sympathetic to me in the building and no hope of anyone coming being able to get in; if I ran upstairs I couldn't get out and by moving I thought that they might hit out at me and I didn't want to die like that. I sat still and said nothing, hoping that Patra would not forget to call for me and that somehow then she would understand the situation and contact the police for me. Patra did come, Patrick let her in without a fuss and then started to shout and swear, saying how wicked I was and how wicked I had been to his 'uncle'. Patra listened to him, the amazement showing on her face, Patrick told her that he thought I should leave the building, she looked questioningly at me, I said that yes I would leave but what could I do with my clothes and furniture as until my house was ready I had nowhere to put them. Patrick said that I should just leave them and he would look after them but he just didn't want me to stay there. I worried about Jasper the cat but he said that he would feed Jasper. With that I was able to leave with Patra. Outside the door I felt a rush of relief and I leapt into the air saying, "Thank goodness you came Patra and thank goodness that I was able to leave with you." "I could tell it was all wrong," said Patra, "and I would have contacted the police straight away if you hadn't come out with me." She worried, "What shall we do now?" I couldn't think seriously about my next move, I knew that I had every right to stay in the building and that I could get legal entry but to be in the building alone with someone like Patrick didn't appeal to me at all. "We planned to see Doris" I said, "Let's do just that, the only thing is I would like a drink." "What coffee or something?" asked Patra. "No, some alcohol is what I need." "Here, take this" she handed me a small parcel "It is liquor chocolates and a miniature bottle of liquor with it." There was in fact two bottles of liquor and I polished them off right there in the street. We went to Kensington to the Commonwealth Institute and Doris' magic tongue and artistry seemed more real than the morning's events. After the show Patra and I went back to her house in Landor Road and sat down to plan my next step. She asked me if I would like to stay with her but she really didn't have that much room. I decided that the best people in this situation would be Kenneth and Sugar, the Barbadian couple that had helped Vincent all those years ago. I telephoned them and they instantly, after hearing my news, invited me to go to them. Leaving Patra I got to Sugar about 11pm. From a horror story morning the night became one of comfort and friendship, by 11-30 I had a bed, clean clothes, and front door keys and was feeling more at home than I had been in the place that should have been safe for me. The next morning I left the house early to go to Clapham so that I could arrange to have my mail redirected. When I reached Balham market I was offered a lift by a young man who used to deliver vegetables to me at the restaurant. I told him what had happened. "I'm sorry about Vincent," he said, "But now maybe I have a chance." "What do you mean?" I asked him. "I have always liked you and get an erection whenever I see you but I was afraid to tell you, but maybe now I can call on you." For the first time I took a good look at this young man, it hadn't occurred to me before that he could like me; he was only about 19 years old and had that dark Mediterranean look. We parked at Clapham Common outside the underground entrance and climbed into the back of the van. With the traffic busy all around us we made love, thoughtfully he had condoms with him. This was my first experience with them, I had thought it would be awkward but found it very natural, at least with this young man. Maybe a new life could be just beginning for me; I had been celibate for so many years. On New Years Eve Beverly was catering for a large dance at Crystal Palace so I went and helped her prepare the food and serve. Ruth was there and so many other Guyanese that I knew, it was a good feeling to start the coming of the New Year amongst friends. Five days later I decided to visit the West Norwood Cemetery to tell Vincent that I was going up to Yorkshire to see my mother. Now that I had no responsibilities with the restaurant or with the cat I was free to go. I left the next day and travelled to Yorkshire on the coach from Victoria. My mother was so pleased to see me as I hadn't been up to see her for some years, we talked a lot about Vincent. She hadn't been surprised that Vincent died saying that when she had spoken to him she somehow knew the end would be soon but anyway, now you can do as you like, you are free again. I stayed with her for about ten days and then went back to my haven in Balham where Sugar and I drank whiskey for breakfast most mornings. It was in the middle of a terrible storm, trees and roofs blowing about in the wind when on the 25th of January I went back to the cemetery to visit Vincent. I took a bottle of whiskey so that together we could celebrate the 40 nights since his death. From there I made my first visit to The Landmark, a centre for people living with HIV, and thought about Vincent a lot. The next day I took over the house in Streatham, I was so pleased and telephoned my mother to tell her about the winter jasmine that was blooming in the garden. It wasn't until the beginning of February that I went back to the restaurant to collect my clothes and some furniture. Patrick made as if he was helping but he was obstructive, I think he had destroyed some of the furniture. Clem and one of his friends helped me to bring my things back to Streatham. The next day I managed to get a telephone number for the young man with the van, he promised to come over during the day but he didn't come. The 6th of February was Vincent's birthday so I went to the cemetery with another bottle of whiskey and had a drink with him, a lot of people telephoned me as if it was my birthday, and I suppose they knew I would be thinking about him. About a week later I learnt from one of Vincent's cousins that he had given her some of his jewellery for her children and asked me if I wanted it back. I told her that if it was his wish then it was my wish as well. I gradually learnt that he had given away most of his personal jewellery to his many godchildren before he went into hospital for the last time. I wished that he had told me.

Finally, 20 days later, the young man with the van came to see me, it was 5am in the morning, he was impulsive but I didn't mind that. Vincent had asked Jan Van Der Knaap to be his executor; Jan visited Patrick and after that decided that he didn't want to be an executor and asked me to take his place. As Vincent had tried to make reparation by making me his main beneficiary, leaving me £80,000, I agreed to do this and had to go to another solicitor to swear an oath. I walked over to the cemetery to tell Vincent what I was doing and to ask him to help me. I still couldn't get used to the idea that he wasn't around to tell me what to do, as he had wanted to do all the years we were together. I was Godfather to the Boateng's youngest boy Seth in place of Vincent; the Methodist Minister asked me how long I had known Vincent and when I told him 28 years he said that he thought it had been a long marriage. In the Caribbean it is customary to expect a dream from someone who dies but it wasn't until the beginning of April that Vincent dreamt me as they say; he told me in the dream that I should live my life now as I couldn't save it up for later. When I told Ruth she laughed and said that Vincent meant that I should find a new friend, adding, of course he wouldn't have told you that when he was alive. Cedric claimed that he also had a will and together with Patrick put caveats on Vincent's will to delay the probate. The first mortgagers protested against the caveats, as until they were lifted they could not proceed with trying to get possession. Since Vincent and Patrick had taken out the new loan not one repayment had been made, the mortgagors were even having to pay for the building insurance. In amongst all this my brother Alan telephoned me to say that my mother had to go to hospital, he wasn't sure what was wrong with her, I told him that I would go back to see her soon. To cheer me up Patra took me to the Chelsea Flower Show, Vincent had gone every year by himself but I had never had either the time or money to go and I really enjoyed the outing. Three days later, the young man with the van came to see me. He brought a vibrator with him, as he wanted to know what it would be like to use it on me. It had been 5 weeks since he last came to visit me, he said he had been on holiday, he had a good tan and did look delicious and I think that the holiday had been his honeymoon. About two weeks later my mother came out of hospital but told me that she didn't feel good at all; I couldn't let her know the truth about my affairs and told her that everything had been settled and that I had no problems. Another week passed and my young man with the van came early in the morning. He said that he had been thinking about me a lot and was very passionate. I asked him if he had got married and he said that he had but that every time he had sex with his wife he had to think about me so that he could satisfy her. Although I missed Vincent a lot I had the thought that God had somehow given me a new life; when I spoke to Cita Pilgrim she invited me to the new official residence in Ealing. I went one Saturday when she was hosting a charity barbecue in aid of the Commonwealth Deaf Aid Society. It was a glittering occasion with all the well-known Guyanese attending. I was able to thank Bernie Grant and Clive Lloyd for their support when Vincent died. I naturally gravitated towards the kitchen and more or less took over the food department and also drank a lot of Guyanese rum, arriving home in an alcoholic haze that was so different to the many times I visited the Lowndes Square apartment at the time when I wasn't drinking and had to make do with orange squash while everyone else drank lots of rum and made lots of noise. When I went up to Shipley in August my mother was very ill and unable to eat. The doctor came while I was there and said that her heart was so weak it was only just beating. When I went with him to the front door he said that he was sorry but there wasn't anything he could do for her, all we could do now was wait. My mother was extremely tired and listless. She didn't like being like that at all; we talked together about death and she said that she was quite prepared and in a way welcomed the prospect. I managed to ask her about my father but the most she would say was that he had been from Essequibo which is the county in Guyana where Vincent had come from; when I asked her his name her memory failed, she was sleepy and I felt I couldn't press her too much then. I was pleased with Alan; he had matured from not being able to boil an egg to being able to care for our mother. I broached the subject of incontinence and he said he was prepared for that as well. I only stayed on for a few more days as my house was empty and I didn't want to leave it for too long. A month later Alan telephoned me to say that our mother was dying, he tried hard not to cry and I couldn't cry, I comforted him and told him that I would return to Shipley as soon as I could. I have an old wooden coat hanger with the name of a dry cleaners in Streatham that hasn't existed for years; pencilled above the shops name is 'Emily', my mother had taken it somewhere and put her name on it. I took out the hanger and spent a long time remembering her, calling her Emily and talking as if she were with me. The next day Alan telephoned to say that she had died, he was calm and said that he would make all the arrangements, she wanted to be cremated and not buried. I felt a need to celebrate and bought some gateaux to share with the people at The Landmark, before going there I visited the cemetery to tell Vincent what had happened. The funeral was so English with everyone trying hard not to cry, only my niece Susan cried and I encouraged her. I had been to the funeral parlour early in the morning to see Emily, she looked so little and frail and when I kissed her and said goodbye I did cry a little then. Afterwards when everyone had left the house Alan and I went through our mother's few papers. I had hoped to find a clue about my father's name but there was nothing there. My stepfather had been another jealous man so I suppose she had thought it wise to destroy any written memories she might have had of another man. In October I went to court together with the mortgagors of the restaurant to get possession legally, Patrick tried to stall again but the mortgagors did obtain possession. Unfortunately by the time we found a buyer the market had fallen dramatically and the price had fallen to £325,000, consequently there wasn't enough to satisfy the outstanding loan so my second charge was worthless and the only thing I got from Vincent's will was the knowledge that he had tried to righten the situation. I consoled myself by hearing again my mother's words

"At least you're free now." I know that I have another chance at life and maybe tomorrow my young man with the van will call.......

ABOUT ME.

Living on a small, more or less non-existent budget my Mother taught me to read at a very early age. By the time I reach 4 years of age I had developed a passion for books and was deep into novels by authors like Ethel M. Dell. At school the only subject that had any interest for me was English and I led the class in classics like The Life Cycle Of A Penny. Later on seeing words jump onto the page from a typewriter fascinated me. Then, after the traumatic events of the 1980's I found that writing gave me a purpose.